T0323991

Cambridge Elements ≡

Elements in Popular Music
edited by
Rupert Till
University of Huddersfield

POPULAR MUSIC IN BRAZIL

Identity, Genres, and Industry

Martha Tupinambá de Ulhôa
Federal University of the State of Rio de Janeiro
Leonardo De Marchi
Federal University of Rio de Janeiro
Renato Pereira Torres Borges
Independent Scholar and Musician

CAMBRIDGE
UNIVERSITY PRESS

Shaftesbury Road, Cambridge CB2 8EA, United Kingdom

One Liberty Plaza, 20th Floor, New York, NY 10006, USA

477 Williamstown Road, Port Melbourne, VIC 3207, Australia

314–321, 3rd Floor, Plot 3, Splendor Forum, Jasola District Centre, New Delhi – 110025, India

103 Penang Road, #05–06/07, Visioncrest Commercial, Singapore 238467

Cambridge University Press is part of Cambridge University Press & Assessment, a department of the University of Cambridge.

We share the University's mission to contribute to society through the pursuit of education, learning and research at the highest international levels of excellence.

www.cambridge.org
Information on this title: www.cambridge.org/9781009565240

DOI: 10.1017/9781009357180

First published 2024

A catalogue record for this publication is available from the British Library.

ISBN 978-1-009-56524-0 Hardback
ISBN 978-1-009-35719-7 Paperback
ISSN 2634-2472 (online)
ISSN 2634-2464 (print)

Popular Music in Brazil

Identity, Genres, and Industry

Elements in Popular Music

DOI: 10.1017/9781009357180
First published online: December 2024

Martha Tupinambá de Ulhôa
Federal University of the State of Rio de Janeiro

Leonardo De Marchi
Federal University of Rio de Janeiro

Renato Pereira Torres Borges
Independent Scholar and Musician

Author for correspondence: Martha Tupinambá de Ulhôa, mulhoa@unirio.br

Abstract: This Element outlines an overview of popular music made in Brazil, from the nineteenth century to the beginning of the twenty-first century. Initially addressing the definition of the "popular" category, discussion then follows on the ways a Brazilian music identity was built after the country's independence in 1822 until the end of the 1920s. An idea of "popular music" was consolidated throughout the twentieth century, from being associated with rural musical performances of oral tradition to the recorded urban musical genres that were established through radio and television. After exploring the world of mass popular music, the relationships between traditional and modern, the topics of cultural diversity, multiculturalism, and the impact of digitalization, as well as the musical kaleidoscope of the twenty-first century, the Element ends with an insight into music genres in the era of digital platforms.

This element also has a video abstract: www.cambridge.org/Martha

Keywords: popular music studies, Brazil, musicology, music history, music genre

ISBNs: 9781009565240 (HB), 9781009357197 (PB), 9781009357180 (OC)
ISSNs: 2634-2472 (online), 2634-2464 (print)

Contents

Overture

Brazilian singer and songwriter Anitta has recently drawn international attention by reaching the top of the Spotify Global Chart, shortly before being nominated for the 2023 Grammy Awards. Previously, other artists and musical genres had stood out in the global music industry, such as *bossa nova* and Tom Jobim, *samba* and Carmen Miranda in the cinema, and even *maxixe* in Paris at the beginning of the twentieth century – to name but a few artists and genres made in Brazil, a country with immense musical diversity and a well-structured music industry.

For the Cambridge Elements series, we will be introducing an overview of popular music in Brazil, addressing not only "typically" Brazilian musical genres (such as samba and bossa nova), but also pop-oriented musical genres (such as rock and electronic music) also produced and consumed in the country. Based on analyses of musicology, history, sociology of culture, and cultural studies, we introduce a new reading of the development of popular music made in Brazil from the nineteenth century to the beginning of the twenty-first century. We understand popular music as urban, modern, registered with and distributed by different information technologies (from sheet music to streaming platforms), and, last but not least, consumed by a heterogeneous audience. However, this is a current notion, since the "popular music" category is a historical concept and, thus, subject to continuous change.

In Brazilian Portuguese, the term "popular music" has different meanings that overlap and/or alternate from one period to another and are closely related to the views and discussions of each time and place, especially those concerning national identity issues.

In the early nineteenth century, "popular" meant "popularity" in the sense of being known (recognized) by many. At times, the term referred to anonymous repertoires of songs and dances and, other times, to specific composers, many of whom were linked to the music theater circuits, with the music performed there often known as "light music." From the late nineteenth century until at least the 1940s, the expression "popular music" was used to refer to music of oral tradition, which was usually anonymous. This is how music with a recreational-religious role and local use was classified – far from commercial use and close to the now seldom used concept of "folk music." This understanding of the expression "popular music" in Brazil is similar to what in French, Italian, and German is known respectively as *musique populaire, musica popolare,* or *populäre Musik,* and is also associated with the working class or folk culture (Middleton, 1990; Scott, 2008).

It was only in the mid twentieth century in Brazil that the notion of modern urban popular music – made and broadcast by the mass media – was consolidated. This understanding of the term, which is close to the widely used "pop music," is relatively recent. It is a type of mass music, close to Anglo-Saxon "pop," and comparable to commercial French popular music, identified as *variétés françaises*, and to the type of sentimental songs currently called *Schlager* in Germany and other countries in Central and Northern Europe.

However, this currently widely accepted conception has not completely replaced the previous notion, since today the expression "popular music" encompasses not only the notion of traditional music orally transmitted (sometimes still called "folk music"), but also industrialized music, made in mass production for a heterogeneous audience. Emerging as a discursive backdrop for this conundrum is the aesthetic and ideological friction between what is artistic ("authentic") and what is commercial, leading to a new version of the "entertainment music vs. serious music" dichotomy that was typical of the nineteenth century.

Accordingly, when dealing with recent commentary that includes this term, it is essential to be mindful of its polysemy. Sometimes, authors adopt the former meaning and, other times, the latter meaning – not to mention the authors who embrace both connotations simultaneously.

In addition to the term's double (or triple) meaning, there is yet another layer when the topic is "popular music" in Brazil: the expression is almost always imbricated in discussions of national identity. This is not a recent issue though; it has been established since the first works on the subject. In the nineteenth century, the concept of "popular" in relation to music meant "popularity," or "known by many," and could indicate music or composers of any nationality. But soon the term "Brazilian" began to identify music considered autochthonous and well-known, and at the end of the century "Brazilian popular" started to be used in connection with folklore studies including in the field of music. Since the beginning of the twentieth century, the historiography of popular music in Brazil has favored narratives associated with identity, gradually developing the idea of a "Brazilian music" lineage based on the so-called "matrices of Brazilian popular music," that is, the *modinha* and *lundu* – genres to which hundreds of studies across the country are dedicated.

During the twentieth century, led by the studies conducted by Mário de Andrade, a large part of music historiography discussed identity issues. Despite the country's immense cultural diversity, the Brazilian popular music historiography has favored the study of musical genres linked to this lineage to the detriment of more comprehensive approaches.

Only recently, since the study of popular music has been disseminated through several areas of knowledge as a result of interdisciplinary dialogues, have musical genres once considered spurious gradually been admitted as a legitimate subject for study. Genres like waltz, polka, *forró* (a lively type of music from the Northeast of Brazil)*, brega* (romantic/cheesy music), black music, *sertanejo* (a type of Brazilian country music), rock, *axé* (Bahian pop music), rap, *manguebeat* (fusion of hard rock with northeastern styles), funk, and rap have gradually emerged. Doors have opened to dances, concerts, and *micaretas* (off-season celebrations of carnival, or "*carnaval*" in Portuguese).

Nonetheless, it is easy to fall into the trap of saying that the (political or aesthetic) boundaries between genres "no longer exist" today, stating that that's how it is now or that the internet has removed the national boundaries of musical genres, for example. In fact, what recent research reveals is that musical flows have always been multicultural. There has always been overlap between musical genres, in addition, of course, to the transatlantic comings and goings of songs made in Brazil. For instance, in the 1960s samba started to be played on drum kits, led by cymbals, something unseen until then; and today's samba includes rhythms (from percussion and singing) from funk, a much younger genre.

While the internet enhances non-territorial musical practices today, this role was once played by television, records, radio, sheet music, instruments, and musicians' tours per se. It was the discourse about such practices, in turn, that often caused – and sometimes still causes – genres to be seen as monolithic and to even be mistaken for being synonymous with national identity. It is easy to notice the international connections between 1960s rock and 1990s mangue-beat, when the discussion about music and nationality had already been established as such. However, one can avoid this trap by going back to the nineteenth century, when newspapers and sheet music listings often showed the waltzes-contradances pair, pointing to a transnational approach *avant la lettre*. Although widely considered Brazilian music today, *xote* has its international connection attested by its correlation to *schottisch*, the dance from which it originated.

Avoiding the term "Brazilian music," we wrote this introduction to popular music *in Brazil* without worrying about omitting musical genres just because their origin was attributed to other countries. We sought, as much as possible, to reflect the musical diversity found in Brazil in a narrative structure that highlights how it intertwines with the music industry and the main aesthetic propositions existing in recent centuries.

This Element comprises three main sections, preceded by an introduction and followed by a conclusion. The Element's subject-matter is developed in a somewhat chronological order, and each section addresses historical and musical aspects related to the various musical genres discussed. The first section deals with how a Brazilian musical identity was built from the country's independence in 1822 to the end of the first two decades of the twentieth century, with relevant comments on music, musicians, instruments, institutions, printing companies, music performance locations, and pioneering music recordings. The second section discusses the consolidation of an idea of popular music throughout the twentieth century, from the notion of "popular" associated with rural musical performances of oral tradition to the recorded urban musical genres that were established through radio and television. The third section explores the world of mass popular music, the relationships between traditional and modern, and the topics of cultural diversity, multiculturalism, the impact of digitalization, and the musical kaleidoscope of the twenty-first century. The Element ends with a coda about musical genres in the era of digital platforms.

1 Building the Idea of Popular and the Music Market in Brazil

This section introduces the development of popular music in Brazil in two overlapping aspects. On the one hand, we discuss how the very idea of *Brazilian* and, later, *popular* music could emerge among the local intelligentsia, in an intellectual and political effort to build a national identity while this Portuguese colony was amid a transformation first into an empire and then into a republic on the American continent. On the other hand, we reconstruct the history of how the music market was set up, from the printing of sheet music to the consolidation of the first record companies at the beginning of the twentieth century.

1.1 The Concepts of Popular Music in the Long Nineteenth Century

Descriptions of musical performances identified as "popular songs" emerged in reports of foreign scientific expeditions made to Brazil in the early nineteenth century. Those descriptions were appropriated by men who took on the mission of creating a specific aspect of the Brazilian Empire in relation to European culture, introducing what they considered to be "Brazilian" music. The two concepts merged toward the end of the nineteenth century, and the notion of "Brazilian popular" was then synonymous with anonymous and predominantly rural traditional musical performances.

The nineteenth-century reference literature for music in Brazil is limited in scope regarding the "popular" repertoire to be discussed. This key reference material appointed certain musical genres as "Brazilian," such as modinha and lundu, omitting several musical genres equally or more present in the daily life of the urban population, such as waltz, polka, and quadrille, which were considered "foreign." In fact, countless musical genres performed throughout the century were neglected, as it is possible to observe in contemporary periodical sources.

In contrast to this limited representation of the "popular" in nineteenth-century Brazil and in order to identify the scope of entertainment music then, we conducted studies using the periodical collection of Hemeroteca Digital Brasileira (HDB, Brazilian Digital Periodicals Library). First, every decade of the nineteenth century was individually explored in a study using the keywords "popular music," "classical music," "serious music," and "light music," in addition to another study dedicated to the 1830–1839 decade, considering the significance of the two genres considered Brazilian in the material, a search for the keywords "modinha" and "lundu/lundum."[1]

In the first half of the nineteenth century, reference was made to "non-Brazilian" genres such as waltzes and contradances and, at the end of the century, to other categories associated with entertainment music, such as *cançoneta*, which, together with modinha and lundu, was later added to the pioneering phonography available in *Discografia Brasileira* (Brazilian Discography, in 78 rpm), hosted on the Instituto Moreira Salles website.[2]

1.1.1 The Brazilian versus the Civilized European: The Emergence of "Popular"

This section discusses essays by representatives of two generations of men of letters in the long nineteenth century in Brazil (Veloso & Madeira, 1999), namely: (1) from the 1830 generation, associated with the Brazilian Historical and Geographical Institute (IHGB, in the acronym in Portuguese), with an article published by Manuel de Araújo Porto-Alegre (1806–1879) in the magazine *Nitheroy*; and (2) from the 1870 generation, associated with the Brazilian Academy of Letters (ABL, in the acronym in Portuguese), with the book *História da literatura brasileira* (Brazilian Literature History), written in 1888, with a second edition in 1902, by Sílvio Romero (1851–1914). Both Porto-Alegre and Romero used the ideas expressed by Carl Friedrich Philipp von Martius (1794–1868) in two works, namely *Travels in Brazil*, written in tandem with Johann Baptist von Spix (1781–1826), and his own essay, "How to Write the History of Brazil," published in 1844 (Ulhôa, 2022).

In the memoirs of their extensive expedition in Brazil between 1817 and 1820, Spix and Martius (2017) describe "popular songs," sung accompanied by the guitar. Those include modinhas, lyrical and sentimental in nature, as well as lundu-songs, some considered lascivious. There, the description of dances qualifies those that are usual in cultured society as "delicate" and "graceful," including lundu, while those danced by the lower classes are described as "sensual" and "unrestrained," with "movements and gestures like those of the negroes."

In 1836, the article "Ideias sobre a música" (Ideas on Music) was published by Araújo Porto-Alegre. It was considered the first, albeit very brief, history of music in Brazil (Kühl, 2014). Porto-Alegre inaugurates a long series of research

---

[1] Search for "Hemeroteca Digital Brasileira." http://memoria.bn.br/hdb/periodico.aspx.
[2] Search for "Discografia Brasileira – Instituto Moreira Salles." Available at: https://discografiabrasileira.com.br/.

on music, involving issues of origins and authenticity vis-à-vis foreign and Brazilian schools. In the aesthetic and ideological perspective, he travels the crossroads of two romantic streams regarding the notion of people: the French, linked to the national, and the German, linked to nature. On the one hand, the character of music composed in Brazil would have been influenced by the environment: lundum, "exceedingly voluptuous, melodic," coming from Bahia in the north of the country, and modinha, "more serious," coming from Minas Gerais in the southern part of the country. On the other hand, in order to underscore the specificity of Brazilian music in comparison with European music, especially Portuguese, and in opposition to theater music (especially Italian opera), Porto-Alegre emphasizes the importance of José Maurício Nunes Garcia (1767–1830), a Brazilian composer of religious and serious music, comparable to Mozart.

Like Spix and Martius, Porto-Alegre identifies social and cultural differences between the types of music performed. At one end were the slaves, playing *marimba*, and, at the other, the masters with their pianos. In the interstices of this social fabric, there was a somewhat marginal urban character, that is, the guitar player.

At the end of the nineteenth century, the "race" category and the positivist view of evolution started to impact the interpretation of music in Brazil, but still in a dialogue with the angle presented by the travelers, including Martius. His historiographic prescription explains that the Brazilian national identity was shaped based on the amalgamation of the three different "races," namely: "the copper-colored or American, the white or Caucasian, and finally the black or Ethiopian." In this triangle, and using a geographical metaphor, "as discoverers, conquerors, and masters, ... the powerful river of Portuguese blood ought to absorb the small tributaries of the Indian and Ethiopian races" (Martius, 1844, p. 382).

In the late nineteenth century, Martius's point of view was expanded by Sílvio Romero, who argued that the history of Brazil should be observed from the perspective of miscegenation. This new racial type, the mestizo, would have overshadowed the two "inferior races" (blacks and reds), which, under the "law of adaptation," would have merged into the former, and, in turn, according to what Romero refers to as the "law of vital competition" would tend to become part of the white Portuguese, a superior race that would predominate (1902, v. 1, p. 89). This spells out the so-called "whitening" theory, which allows miscegenation, but still considers it a "stain" that should be blamed for Brazil's late development of its civilization.

Despite focusing on literature, Romero speaks of "Brazilian," "anonymous," and "endangered" music, as traditional orally transmitted music was considered at the time. Thus, he simply alludes to modinhas, square dances (*quadrille*), marches, sacred music, and fantasia, which he knew firsthand, in Sergipe, his home state (1902, v. 1, p. 321). He distinguishes two types of music: one "with a lyrical, light, fleeting, and mild character, or music of the streets, music of the people; the other more serious and demure, or church music" (p. 374). The few names mentioned in relation to music were the lettered romantic composers, including José Maurício Nunes Garcia, precursor of Henrique Alves de Mesquita (1830–1906), author of operettas and *féeries* (or fairy plays), and Antonio Carlos Gomes (1836–1896), a follower of Verdi and just as "popular" as the Italian opera composer.

1.1.2 Disputes over the Meaning of "Popular"

As previously mentioned, the variety of existing musical genres is not in the scope of studies by the men of letters discussed so far, such is their diligence in distinguishing the element of identity in the face of European culture in the profane music performed in Brazil. In advertisements for sheet music for sale in Rio de Janeiro, next to the label "modinhas" one can see several contradances (quadrille), most of them for piano, but also for flute, in addition to countless waltz collections. This shows that there was a demand for music to be used by amateurs, which demonstrates how the entertainment industry in Brazil started to be built.

In nineteenth-century periodicals in Brazil, the idea of "popular" implied being known or recognized by many, whether referring to anonymous repertoires of songs and dances, or to specific composers, many of whom were linked to musical theater circuits (the "popular Offenbach"). Also, the music performed then was also known as "light music." Perhaps this is why some researchers use the term "light" as synonymous with "popular." However, by reading the periodicals, one may determine that, at least in the nineteenth century, "light music" relates to musical theater (operettas, comic operas, vaudevilles, and féeries) as opposed to classical music.[3]

As for the "Brazilian" music categories, modinha and lundu (or lundum) appear both in theatrical performances, many of which for the benefit of a musician, and in compositions listed for sale. The following advertisement, posted in *Jornal do Commercio*, is representative of this. In addition to showing the search terms, it contextualizes musical performances in the theater. It is a "benefit" performance, that is, the proceeds from the sale of tickets went to the two actors on stage and to the members of *Sociedade do Teatro Imperial* (Imperial Theater Society). Also, the event is identified as "entertainment," pointing to its "lighthearted" character. Finally, note the expression "in black character," a stereotyped characterization of

---

[3] For example, please refer to: *Semana Ilustrada*, n. 34, p. 2, August 4, 1861. http://memoria.bn.br/DocReader/702951/266.

the African cultural matrix in Brazilian culture, which is similar to black-face, a quite widespread practice in the international musical theater at that time.

> TEATRO CONSTITUCIONAL FLUMINENSE / Saturday, May 18, 1833, for the benefit of the actors and members, Maria Cândida Vaconni and Manoel Alves. [To be performed, among other acts] "O Dueto" (The Duet) and "**Lundum** do Alfaiate" (The Tailor's Lundum) by the beneficiaries [and] "**Modinhas Brasileiras**" (Brazilian Modinhas) by the beneficiary **in black-face**. Rounding off the **entertainment**, the new and playful farce called "O BACHAREL EM FÉRIAS, ou as sete pitadas." (THE BACHELOR ON VACATION, or the seven pinches). / Sociedade do Teatro Imperial (Imperial Theater Society). (*Jornal do Commercio*, n. 113, p. 3, May 14, 1833). (Emphasis added)

Most advertisements included national identification categories, even on a limited basis, together with songs from the most varied sources, mainly Iberian (both Portuguese and Spanish), as well as many adaptations of Italian and French entertainment songs introduced by opera and vaudeville companies that toured in Rio de Janeiro (Magaldi, 2004). The songs that were successful in the theater were soon published in simplified versions for singing and piano. Publications ranged from the remarkable example of the collection *Delícias da Traviata* (Delights of La Traviata), which gave the arias from Verdi's *Traviata* new lyrics in Portuguese, to works created by Brazilian artists, such as the repertoire of lundus and modinhas by Xisto Bahia (1841–1894). "Yayá, você quer morrer" (Girl, You Want to Die) is the title used in the sheet music arranged by an anonymous musician ("Arrangement by XXX," as shown in the original sheet music) of the lundu "Isto é bom" (This is Good), from Bahia's repertoire, later recorded by Casa Edison in 1902.[4]

The various differentiations of musical genres often contrast the categories relating to "erudite" music, as artistic and lettered, and to "popular" music, of written or oral transmission, as is the case with the salon modinha (usually for singing and piano) and street modinha (for singing and guitar) (Tupinambá de Ulhôa, 2020). At the end of the nineteenth century, the street modinhas had a great boost due to the activity of instrumentalists, composers, lyricists, and singers performing in Rio de Janeiro in *choro* groups, which, in addition to playing at all kinds of family events, played in serenades, often waking up residents of several houses and leading to impromptu parties.

Those choro musicians ended up being responsible for the process of adapting the dance genres that arrived in Brazil in the nineteenth century to create the genres that would later be recorded on records and broadcast on the radio,

---

[4] The sheet music for Xisto Bahia's "Iaiá você quer morrer" is available at the International Music Score Library Project (IMSLP): https://imslp.org/wiki/Iai%C3%A1_voc%C3%AA_quer_morrer_(Bahia%2C_Xisto). The phonograms for "Isto é bom" are discussed in Section 1.2.2.

representing the so-called twentieth-century "urban popular music." This appropriation process took place not only in Rio de Janeiro, as recorded in the hegemonic historiography, but also in other cities, especially in the capitals of the provinces that were placed along the Atlantic coast (Costa Neto, 2015). In the nineteenth century, there was an intense traffic of musicians mostly from the north and northeast of the country to Rio de Janeiro, where, in fact, the publishing houses were located.

Many professional musicians played "by ear," but most were musically literate. In his book *O choro*, published in 1936, Alexandre Gonçalves Pinto conducted a survey of "old-school" musicians performing in Rio de Janeiro since 1870. Pedro Aragão (2015), after reviewing Pinto's book vis-à-vis several musical collections, concluded that the choro repertoire was also transmitted in written form. It should be noted that they were professional musicians coming from music bands, where they learned (and still learn) music notation.

Two artists stand out in this world of emerging urban popular music – the poet-composer Catulo da Paixão Cearense (1863–1946) and the clown-singer Eduardo das Neves (1874–1919). The former recorded his extensive production of lyrics for modinhas in songbooks, many of them adapted to existing musical works. The latter, in addition to compiling traditional lundus and cançonetas, recorded compositions about the political, cultural, and behavioral novelties of the time (Martins, 2022). These "popular songbooks" – with song lyrics – represented an important segment of the music publishing market in Rio de Janeiro.

Other places that hosted urban popular music in Rio de Janeiro were public festivals such as carnival (in February) or Festa da Penha (Penha Festival) (in October). New compositions or new versions of traditional songs were often tested at Festa da Penha, so that they would have been memorized by revelers by carnival time.

One of these 1914 carnival hits was "Cabocla de Caxangá," which inspired a group of musicians, including Pixinguinha (1897–1973), Donga (1890–1974), and João Pernambuco (João Teixeira Guimarães, 1883–1947), to put together a carnival group, the Grupo do Caxangá, which remained active until 1919, when part of the musicians started to create the group Oito Batutas.

"Cabocla de Caxangá" is a good example of how to turn a song that clearly originated from oral tradition into a popular "commercial" song.[5] The *embolada* (a fast song with a short chorus and verses with many words, hence the "embolada" – or tangling – of the lyrics) was part of João Pernambuco's repertoire, according to a testimonial from Pixinguinha, but it received verses

---

[5] Several authors discuss this song, especially regarding issues of authorship and alleged plagiarism, as well documented by Daniella Thompson. Please refer to: http://daniellathompson.com/Texts/Le_Boeuf/cron.pt.17.htm.

and was registered by Catulo da Paixão Cearense in one of his many songbooks (*Lyra dos Salões*, 1913). In recordings, the various versions are labeled from *batuque sertanejo* (Odeon 120.521) to *tango* (Odeon 120.947), to *toada* (Odeon 120.954) and *cançoneta* (Gaúcho R 766), as well as maxixe (*Diário de Pernambuco*, n. 234, p. 11, Sep. 24, 1914).

Periodicals published as of 1914 reported several different lyrics to be sung to the tune of "Cabocla de Caxangá," including two anthems of competing carnival groups. The piano sheet music is available at the International Music Score Library Project (IMSLP).[6] The document has a stamp from the distributing store (Casa Mozart, Rio de Janeiro) and, on the left side of the score, the label printed for the genre classifies the song as "samba." It also shows the catalog number of Carlos Wehrs publishing house (C.W. 417) and, quite revealingly, an indication that the score was owned by Fred Figner, who bought the rights to virtually all entertainment sheet music in Rio de Janeiro, much of which was recorded by Casa Edison.

1.2 Development of the Music Market (1820–1920)

The Brazilian music market in Brazil started to be developed in the nineteenth century. The key triggering event for this was the transfer of the Portuguese royal court to the city of Rio de Janeiro. Fleeing from the Napoleonic army invasions, the Portuguese royal family decided to relocate to Brazil with part of the royal court and arrived in the colony in 1808. Once established in Rio de Janeiro, the royal family decided, in 1815, to turn the city into the capital of the United Kingdom of Portugal, Brazil, and the Algarves.

As they settled in the kingdom's new capital, the Portuguese court invested in creating institutions dedicated to the arts, notably to music. King João VI (who reigned from 1816 to 1822) ordered the construction of Teatro da Ópera (Opera House) and of Capela Real de Música (Music Royal Chapel) in accordance with Portuguese musical performance standards (Bernardes, 2006; Cardoso, 2008; Monteiro, 2008). At the same time, the troubled period of the Napoleonic Wars contributed to attracting European musicians to Rio de Janeiro. Not only Portuguese musicians arrived in the country, as was the case with Marcos Portugal (1762–1830), but also the renowned Austrian composer and pianist Sigismund von Neukomm (1778–1858), a disciple of Haydn. He worked at the court of King João VI, as well as the Belgian flutist Mathieu-André Reichert, who was responsible for introducing the modern Boehm transverse flute system during the reign of King Pedro II (1840–1889) (Cazes, 1999; Dias, 1990). During the time of the monarchy, this cultural effort became more systematic,

---

[6] See: https://imslp.org/wiki/File:PMLP971894-Cabocla_de_caxang%C3%A1.pdf.

with scholarships being granted at music institutes in Europe to Brazilian musicians, and the opening of the first Music Conservatory in 1848.

1.2.1 Music Press and Modern Instruments

Upon their relocation to Rio de Janeiro, the Portuguese crown took measures to meet administrative demands, which allowed the flourishing of two key businesses for a music market: the printing of sheet music and the sale of modern musical instruments.

The Royal Press decree of 1808 allowed the private production of printed material in Brazil, an activity then limited, however, to the State. According to Mônica Leme (2006), it was only with the Royal Charter of 1811 that the existence of private typographies was allowed. Since then, there have been records of the development of commercial production of sheet music, the first being printed in 1813 by the Portuguese typographer Manuel Antônio da Silva Serva, based in Salvador da Bahia. According to the *Enciclopédia da Música Brasileira* (1998, p. 370–379), although it was possible to find printers producing material related to music during the 1820s, it was only in 1834 that the Frenchman Pierre Laforge opened "Estamparia de Música" (music printing shop), thus becoming the first systematic printer of musical scores in Rio de Janeiro. From the 1840s onward, dozens of establishments of music publishers and printers were established in the city of Rio de Janeiro and in other capitals of the country. In addition to sheet music (many of them written in a simplified form, to expand the consumer market), songbooks with the lyrics of modinhas and lundus emerged. Catulo da Paixão Cearense stood out among the song compilers for having coordinated as many as 15 of these compilations, some of them with repeated editions (Leme, 2006).

At the same time, the consumption of modern instruments by individuals was growing. Historians like Marcos Napolitano (2002) and Mônica Leme (2006) state that the hosting of balls by the Portuguese court in the 1840s gave rise to an appreciation of evening house parties (so-called *soirées*) and to the learning of musical instruments by the wealthiest families, especially pianos, but also the guitar across the middle and lower classes. The elites of the new imperial capital sought to obtain modern instruments as a means to display a level of "civility" that was consistent with the new political order. José Ramos Tinhorão (2012) notes that the acquisition of these instruments increased to such an extent among the Rio de Janeiro elite that the intellectual Manuel de Araújo Porto-Alegre even said, in 1856, that Rio had become the "city of pianos."

The association of the soirée fad and the publication of sheet music set the conditions for the development of a music market: the interest in playing modern instruments implied learning performance techniques and reading music, which demanded both the purchase of sheet music and hiring teachers of the instruments. This allowed professional musicians to publish their works in sheet music, give classes, and perform in concert halls and venues, receiving financial compensation for their work.

At the same time, the urban transformations in the capital of the empire allowed the emergence of new types of musical venues, such as clubs and vaudevilles, which conceptually combined drinking, eating, and dancing, thus resulting in a new type of entertainment (Diniz, 2007; Leme, 2006; Tinhorão, 2012). These venues would have been responsible not only for the introduction of new European musical genres – which would soon reinforce the repertoire of dance-able songs – but would also serve as a place for lay musicians to learn and work.

1.2.2 Echoes of Modernity: Talking Machines in the Tropics

The existence of a European royal court in the tropics also allowed the Rio de Janeiro elite to gain easier access to innovative mechanical technologies for reproducing sounds in the nineteenth century.[7] The newspapers of the 1820s on mention the first mechanical music playing technologies, such as music boxes and, especially, barrel organs, revealing how familiar certain circles of the Rio de Janeiro society were with these new technologies (Ulhôa & Costa-Lima Neto, 2015; Ulhôa, 2021). The technologies smoothed the way for the *fin de siècle* audience to develop their sensitivity to an even more disruptive technology: the phonograph. Music boxes and barrel organs were the first instruments that set musical performance apart from its original ritualistic context (masses, popular festivals, rituals, etc.), introducing the figure of the listener through what historian Marialva Barbosa (2013) labeled as *imperfect mediations*, that is, a process of singularization and domestication of the mediated sounds vis-à-vis the performative context.

The first phonographs were introduced in Rio de Janeiro in the 1880s (Franceschi, 2002). However, it was at the turn of the twentieth century that a systematic production of sound recordings and the sale of records began to establish in the country.

The history of Brazil's phonographic industry began at the turn of the twentieth century, when the European merchant Frederico (Fred) Figner (1866–1947) arrived in Rio de Janeiro. Figner was born in a region that belonged to the Austro-Hungarian Empire (part of the Czech Republic today) and emigrated to the

---

[7] Authors like Friedrich Kittler (1999), Jonathan Sterne (2003), Lisa Gitelman (1999), and Paul Théberge (1999) note that such mechanical technologies for reproducing sounds result from an epistemological revolution that began to understand the human senses as a mechanical key. This led to the emergence of numerous sound *reproducing* technologies, from the music box to the telephone.

United States at the end of the nineteenth century, where he acquired phonographs to tour with the new device across Latin America. After arriving in the city of Belém, Pará state, in 1891, Figner traveled extensively throughout Brazil introducing the phonograph. In 1898, he decided to live in Rio de Janeiro, where he opened a store that sold imported manufactured goods, Casa Edison (named after Thomas A. Edison). The store offered a variety of products brought from industrialized countries, such as ink pens and typewriters, in addition to *talking machines*, as phonographs and gramophones were then popularly referred to. From 1900 on, Figner would import records recorded in Europe and the United States. The business was so successful that, in 1902, the Brazil-based entrepreneur signed a contract with the International Zonophone Company, headquartered in Germany, for the production of double-sided records recorded in his store in Rio de Janeiro.

Considering that the contract between Figner and Zonophone stipulated that the former would select artists and repertoire (A&R), he went ahead and hired local musicians and songwriters to perform all genres of music. He recorded the Band of the [Rio de Janeiro] Fire Department, conducted by Anacleto de Medeiros, as well as flutist Patápio Silva and pianists (and music composers) Chiquinha Gonzaga and Ernesto Nazareth, among other artists from the city's music scene.[8] In quantitative terms, Figner soon became one of the largest disc producers in the world, after the United States, Germany, and the United Kingdom.

In his dissertation on the configurations of Brazilian songs, Judson Lima (2013) studies the catalogs of Casa Edison. He notes that the label "Repertório de modinhas" (Repertoire of Modinhas) includes "Canções cantadas e acompanhadas ao violão por Cadete" (Songs Sung and Accompanied on the Guitar by Cadete) and "Cançonetas e Lundus" (Cançonetas and Lundus) by "popular Brazilian songwriter Bahiano." In the 1902 catalog, there were 81 cançonetas and lundus, 50 modinhas, 16 polkas, 9 waltzes, 7 *dobrados*, 6 duets, 5 tangos, 5 maxixes, and 4 marchas (Franceschi, 2002, p. 85–100). One may infer that an umbrella label (modinhas) was established, encompassing (sentimental) "songs," (theatrical) "cançonetas," and (satirical) "lundus."

An example of lundu from the turn of the century is the song "Isto é bom" (This is good), attributed to the composer and performer Xisto Bahia. The structure of the song suggests that it was an improvisation, since it is structured only as a short chorus with two sentences – "Isto é bom, Isto é bom que dói!" (This is good, this is so good it hurts!) – and verses without an apparent narrative order. According to Ulhôa (2011), each of the recorded versions, as well as their

---

[8] Virtually everything that is available on pioneering mechanical recordings can be found in the online collection *Discografia Brasileira* (DB) of *Instituto Moreira Salles*.

respective sheet music, has a different melody, but all are based on the chorus, which is what identifies the song. It is thus suggested that it is a "popular" song of oral/aural transmission.

In 1908, the Italian brothers Savério and Emilio Leonetti opened a record store – Discos Gaúcho – in the city of Porto Alegre, in the south of Brazil. Their aim was to compete with Figner not only in the Brazilian market, but also in Argentina and Uruguay, thanks to the proximity of the state of Rio Grande do Sul. (Franceschi, 2002; Vedana, 2006).

While the competition was being established, Figner began to expand his business across Brazil, opening branches of Casa Edison in other cities or entering into partnerships with other record stores (such as Casa Hartlieb, in Porto Alegre). In 1911, Figner started negotiations to build a record factory in Rio de Janeiro. At that time, the company he worked with – International Talking Machine-Odeon – had been acquired by the Carl Lindström record label. In view of the imminence of what would become the First World War, European businessmen sought to protect their capital by building record factories outside Europe. Figner was selected as the business partner responsible for overseeing the construction of these facilities in Latin America. The Odeon record factory opened in 1913 and was the first of its kind in South America[9] (Franceschi, 2002). In 1914, the Leonetti brothers also opened their factory – A Elétrica – in Porto Alegre. Although theirs was a smaller facility than the one in Rio de Janeiro, one should not ignore the fact that Brazil had, in the mid-1910s, two pioneer record factories in South America, which turned it into the subcontinent's great record manufacturing center.

The end of the 1920s, however, inaugurated another phase for the music industry structure. When patents for music reproducing devices became public domain, competition between record companies began to be mediated by the curation of catalogs. This encouraged direct investment by companies from industrialized countries in markets around the world. Between 1928 and 1930, Columbia Records, RCA-Victor, and Brunswick began to operate directly in the country.

The reorganization of the international economy after the end of the First World War was another important change in the market structure. While American, British, German, Italian, and Japanese companies competed for new markets before the war, the record companies with headquarters in the defeated countries lost protagonism in the international market. In 1919, for example, the Lindström group became the Transoceanic Trading Company. In 1925, the

---

[9] Figner was also responsible for overseeing the construction of another company factory in Buenos Aires, Argentina. The facility opened in 1919.

company was acquired by London-based Columbia Graphophone, which would be the backbone, as of 1931, of Electric and Musical Industries (EMI).

From 1926, the English investors began to demand a direct involvement in the Brazilian subsidiary (Franceschi, 2002). The English company has gradually taken control of the catalogs of Brazil-based Odeon, having acquired the copyright of works already recorded. Then they demanded the right to manage the company's production, including the A&R department. Finally, a new contract review in 1932 forced Figner to hand over the Rio de Janeiro factory to them. Figner even tried to stay in the music business as an independent producer, but he failed.

2 The Social Construction of Music as Popular and Brazilian: Aesthetics, Ideology, and Politics (1920–2000)

This section addresses how the concept of *popular* music and *Brazilian* music was built from an aesthetic, intellectual, and political perspective. The twentieth century posed a number of challenges for artists and intellectuals who were dedicated to thinking about the culture of Brazil. From a purely aesthetic point of view, the emergence of mass culture made the definition of what would be authentically *popular* music more complex: the folkloric sense of the term was challenged by the commercial meaning of the word, with *popular* being what was most listened to among the emerging urban masses. This movement generated a long discussion about aesthetics among intellectuals not only from the Brazilian modernist movement – when the figure of Mário de Andrade would assume a leading role in the debate on music in Brazil – but also to the left-wing intellectuals who, faced with the creation of a cultural industry, would turn to critical theory to differentiate what would be a truly *national-popular* culture from an *international-popular* culture. This debate was also permeated by several movements that, over the course of a century, transformed the political scene.

With the rise of Getúlio Vargas to power in 1930, there was an effort to turn the cultural manifestations of the city of Rio de Janeiro into the symbol of a *Brazilian nation*. This was when samba gained prominence over other musical genres as the synthesis of *Brazilian popular music*. This narrative would be further established by the works of the musicians and intellectuals around bossa nova (BN) and, later, the so-called Brazilian Popular Music (MPB). After the downfall of the military dictatorship (1964–1985), there was a greater political effort to create a cultural industry in the country that would generate an international-popular aesthetic that hopefully would replace the popular-national music championed by left-wing intellectuals and artists. At the end of the years of dictatorship, Brazilian music had established traditional genres (such as samba, BN and MPB) that conversed with pop musical genres (rock, soul, post-punk), becoming one of the most important record markets in the world. In short, it ended up defining what would be popular music and Brazilian music, opening a wide outlook on the aesthetic hybridizations that emerged in the century that followed.

2.1 Nationalist Modernism

The project to define Brazilian music continued into the twentieth century around nationalist modernism. There were two instances and two notions of popular: first, in the 1920s, when Mário de Andrade proposed an alliance between classical composers and the folkloric legacy, in counterpoint to the influence of urban popular music, which was considered to be disruptive (Wisnik, 2022, p. 175); and the second instance, triggered by the BN movement and radicalized by the Tropicalists in the urban popular music of the 1960s, when Brazilianness was sought not only in the traditional, but also in the urban and global (Campos, 1974; Elias, 2015; Zan, 1997). It was only in the 1970s that the modern notion of popular music was consolidated, especially in the writings of José Ramos Tinhorão (1928–2021), who defined it as an urban phenomenon that emerged in middle-class cities, with acknowledged authorship and written or recorded transmission (2013, p. 9). The notion of popular as "pop" or "mass" would only establish itself in the 1990s, as discussed further in the third section.

2.1.1 The First Modernist Wave and the Concept of Brazilian Music

At the beginning of the twentieth century, the figure that stands out in the historiography of music in Brazil is the polymath Mário de Andrade (1893–1945). He was the mentor of the so-called "nationalist modernism" movement, whereby the search for a renewal of musical art by erudite composers should involve an immersion in traditional culture as inspiration and material source (rhythms, melodies, forms, timbres) for musical creation.

Andrade himself tried to fulfill what he called the "Brazilian artist's mission" by collecting (either personally or receiving from collaborators), transcribing, organizing, and mainly writing and teaching about the musical characteristics of what he called "Brazilian folk," that is, folk music traditions, including modinha (sentimental songs) and lundu (critical-satirical or risqué songs).

The role played by Andrade was prominent, mainly through his program-matic and didactic essay *Ensaio sobre a música brasileira* (Essay on Brazilian Music), published in 1928, with four re-publishings and numerous reprints and a commented critical edition in 2020. The impact of Ensaio transcended the circle of concert music composers for which it had been initially designed and served as a textbook for generations of conservatory students, as well as a reference source about the history of popular music in Brazil for researchers and musicians, including several authors and enthusiasts.

Mário de Andrade's impact was even more felt in literature, which may explain his great intellectual influence. It is remarkable that he used, in the creative process of his literary work entitled *Macunaíma, o herói sem caráter* (Macunaíma, The Hero with No Character), also published in 1928, the compositional process of the traditional music described in Ensaio, that is, the rhapsodic principle of the suite – a collection of dances with contrasting tempos sharing the same key – and the form of theme and variations (Mello e Souza, 2003).

Both Ensaio and Macunaíma have ultimately been included in the Brazilian imagery, contributing to the emergence of a type of "monoculturalism" (Napolitano, 2022), that is, a unanimous acceptance both by the right-wingers (as a "colonial heritage to be preserved") and the left-wingers ("as a vocation for racial and cultural fusion in the creation of a classism-based "national-popular" culture"). Despite the different political perspectives, there was a certain consensus about a "long-term modernism" in Brazil, which began with the historical landmark represented by the 1922 Week of Modern Art and lasted until the 1980s, oriented around a general feeling of "brasilidade" (Brazilianness) based on racial miscegenation and the search for a cultural language that was common to all races and classes.

While Mário de Andrade established the theoretical foundations for Brazilian nationalism in the twentieth century, it was Villa-Lobos (1887–1959) who fulfilled the modernist aspirations in the musical field (Neves, 2008). Except for certain "lapses" of easy exoticism, Mário de Andrade, in the role of critic, often praises Villa Lobos's ability to produce "phenomenal" music, like his *Choros*, a number of compositions inspired by musical practices associated with carnival and to street musician performances in Rio de Janeiro. Among them is *Choros no. 10*, for symphony orchestra and mixed choir. The second part of the work features the song "Rasga o Coração" (Tear Your Heart), which became its subtitle. This has the melody of "Yara," a schottisch by Anacleto de Medeiros (1866–1907), whose lyrics were added by Catulo da Paixão Cearense, already mentioned in the previous section as a mediator between oral culture and audible culture.[10]

As regards choro, Villa-Lobos influenced many popular music composers, especially with the series of *Serestas* (Serenades), from the 1920s, such as the

---

[10] Both "Yara" and "Rasga o Coração" were recorded by Casa Edison in 1904 and 1909, respectively, and are available for listening on the Brazilian Discography (https://discografiabrasileira.com.br/fonograma/2618/iara and https://discografiabrasileira.com.br/fonograma/7219/iara-rasga-o-coracao.

duo Antônio Carlos Jobim (1927–1994) and Vinicius de Moraes (1913–1980), and Edu Lobo (1943–) and Chico Buarque de Hollanda (1944–), members of an intermediate category that was "intellectualized, but not academic; popular, but not folkloric." This group of composers wrote songs in the modinha lineage but associated with a type of modern musical "Brazilianness" that was far from Andrade's modernist nationalism (Dias, 2017).

Mário de Andrade's ideological bias has long been outdated. However, his musicological insights remain valid, such as his discussion of the so-called "characteristic syncope." According to him, this rhythm appears above all in the performance, since traditional notation does not do it justice. Andrade's examples are the maxixes and sambas by Sinhô (José Barbosa da Silva, 1888–1930) – ordinary on the sheet music, but "extraordinary and superb" in the recorded performances, "the melodies being transfigured by the new rhythms" (Andrade, 2020, p. 72).

2.1.2 Sinhô, Bountman, and Mário Reis – The First Modernization Phase of Samba

Parallel to Mário de Andrade's musicological collection and analysis of traditional music in Brazil, journalist Francisco Guimarães – also known as Vagalume (Firefly) (c. 1875–1946) – published, in 1933, the book *Na roda de samba* (In the Samba Circle), with chronicles that address the refinement process of samba, from its rural and "rustic" roots (country-like sound and accent) in Bahia to its variants (*samba raiado* and *samba corrido*) to its "civilized" development (*samba chulado*, with rhyming lyrics and full of melody). These types of samba migrated to Rio de Janeiro and were played, along with the so-called *partido alto* offshoot (with short choruses and improvised verses), in samba circles (*rodas de samba*) that gathered enthusiasts in the homes of the so-called *tias* or "aunts." The tias were women, many of them priestesses of African religious groups, that systematically opened their houses for the evening parties with music. Vagalume may have been the first to report the existence of Tia Ciata's house, where "Pelo telefone" (Over the Phone) was collectively created with lyrics about everyday events and using a traditional song as its chorus. Donga, one of the participants, registered the carnival samba "Pelo telefone" at the National Library as his own, inaugurating, according to the author, the "samba industry," that is, turning music into a profitable commodity for its authors and publishers.

Vagalume describes the samba creation and recognition process: it would start on the *morros* (the hills that surround the city of Rio de Janeiro), then be submitted for consideration by a samba circle (like those at Tia Ciata's house), and, if approved, it would be transmitted orally "by word of mouth." He had many restrictions on samba being recorded on records, but describes with awe what he called the "tricks" used by Sinhô to pave the way for samba to gain access to other places in addition to the samba circles.

According to the journalist, the "King of Samba" used various methods to accomplish this – whether by making a pianist lover play his songs in sheet music shops; by offering his production arranged for music bands at carnival clubs; by having his songs played daily on the piano at the "cheerful boarding houses"; or for being acknowledged as a composer for the theater. From the vaudevilles (revues), his songs were then "easily released in Penha amidst a resounding success."

Sinhô easily and skillfully adapted the traditional composition model for larger consumption. He noticed that the change in the musical production structure was beginning to be rationalized and he invested heavily in the production and promotion of his compositions, whether in theaters, on records, or by training a singer suited to the new configuration (as he did with Mário Reis, one of his best interpreters and precursor of the bossa-nova style of singing).

The recordings at the end of the 1920s are emblematic and show how Sinhô, among the old-school composers, was the one who walked the furthest along the path of samba's transformations (Sandroni, 2012). Sinhô wrote songs more suited to the new format sought by the record industry: a product with technical and musical quality that could interest a larger audience, going beyond the artisanal world and linked to the daily life of local neighborhoods and people, religion, or leisure. To this end, he was supported by musician Simon Bountman (1900–1977), who had extensive experience in the entertainment music business and arranged and participated in the recordings of several tracks by Sinhô for Casa Edison (Giron, 2001).

Those include two versions of "Jura" (Promise), both with the same arrangement, written on the same day, but recorded with different microphones settings in order to produce two different balances between instruments and vocals. In the first version, featuring Mário Reis and his soft voice, the piano blends with the other instruments, while in the second, featuring singer-actress Aracy Cortes in a higher tonality, the piano stands out to make up for her sharper and more cutting tone.[11] The arrangement accurately follows the sheet music edited by Sinhô both for the 1928 and 2000 versions, with the latter being sung by Zeca Pagodinho (Jessé Gomes da Silva Filho, b. 1959), when "Jura" was the theme song of a soap opera broadcast on prime time television.

---

[11] Both versions of "Jura," with Mário Reis, and Aracy Cortes, as well as the original score are available online at the International Music Score Library Project (IMSLP) / Petrucci Music Library. See: https://imslp.org/wiki/Jura!_(Sinh%C3%B4).

2.2 In Search of Popular, Urban, and Brazilian Music (1930–1960)

From the late 1920s onward, patenting ceased to be the regulatory mechanism for the record industry. Former alliances between local producers (record labels) and international producers (record factories) were replaced by direct investments from foreign capital (De Marchi, 2016). In 1922, radio began to develop rapidly in the country, with the emergence of stations that also broadcast songs (Calabre, 2004). A mediatic ecosystem between record companies and radio stations started to develop.

In 1930, there was a coup d'état led by dissident factions of the local elites, putting an end to the so-called First Republic and lifting the caudillo Getúlio Vargas (1882–1954) into command. In order to dismantle the supremacy of the previous ruling elites, the interim government of Vargas promoted a bureaucratic and symbolic centralization of power in the then capital of the republic, the city of Rio de Janeiro. One of his first acts as president was the burning of the state flags, indicating that the *national* flag should prevail over them. The same center-driven spirit was replicated in the arts: Vargas began to promote cultural expressions that were to be defined as national (that is, hierarchically superior to regional manifestations). A policy of valuing cultural expressions from Rio de Janeiro (i.e., the Carioca culture) began as part of a narrative about Brazil (Vianna, 2004). Local cultural expressions started to be appreciated on a national level: *feijoada* in cuisine, carnival in popular festivals, and Afro-Brazilian dance songs, such as the emerging samba (Sandroni, 2012).

In 1937, Vargas staged another coup d'état, establishing a fascist-style dictatorship known as Estado Novo (1937–1945). During that period, the effort to create national symbols grew stronger, with the establishment of government agencies to orchestrate this process. The measures included the nationalization of Rádio Nacional, a radio station that became the official government radio station but with a commercial format (Saroldi & Moreira, 1988). The radio programming was about entertainment, having news, radio soap operas, and music as its main products. Supported by financial and political capital, Rádio Nacional hired several composers, arrangers, and singers, becoming the main agent of the music economy in the period. Through the work of *maestros* (bandleaders) such as Pixinguinha and Radamés Gnattali (1906–1988), a set of standard arrangements for popular music was produced in radio stations to be used on radio and in records, featuring a certain type of sound. Counting on the Estado Novo campaigns, popular music from Rio de Janeiro began to be valued as urban (modern) and Brazilian (national) popular music, surpassing other musical expressions.

With the Second World War, the rapport between the United States and Brazil made Brazilian cultural products spread through the American cultural industry: Carmen Miranda (1909–1955) moved to Hollywood, becoming the Brazilian Bombshell, and Walt Disney created the character *Zé Carioca* (Joe Carioca), a parrot who drinks *cachaça*, plays the *tamborim*, and dances to the samba (Santos, 2019). In the postwar period, bossa nova consolidated this Brazil-United States relationship through music, solidifying an imagery of Brazil that was intermingled with the musicality of Rio de Janeiro. *Samba carioca* (samba from Rio de Janeiro) started to play a major role in the historiography of music in Brazil, inaugurating a lineage of canonical genres, which includes bossa nova from the 1950s and MPB from the 1960s.

2.2.1 Modern Samba – The Estácio Paradigm

As mentioned by Carlos Sandroni (2012), the history of samba in Rio de Janeiro is associated with the existence of two successive samba styles, with the first style being etched in recordings made from 1917 (the year of the hit "Pelo Telefone") to the late 1920s, and the second being recorded as of the 1930s, when the samba of that time met its modern version. Based on his experience as a guitar player, Sandroni studies the accompaniment patterns for the two samba styles by examining sheet music and recordings.

The accompaniment for "old" sambas, including those by Sinhô, as already mentioned, as well as for maxixe, lundu, and habanera, is based on rhythmic cells that were usual in the nineteenth-century South American dance songs, including the cell that Mário de Andrade referred to as "characteristic syncopation" and the *tresillo*, or clave, in Cuban music. These accompaniment patterns are linked to what Sandroni called the "tresillo paradigm" (Figure 1), as they involve three asymmetrical articulations in an eight-pulse cycle creating the 3+3+2 rhythmic pattern, found in several oral tradition songs in Brazil as well as in the hand claps that accompany the Bahian samba de roda (samba raiado, already mentioned), *coco do nordeste*, and the partido-alto samba in Rio de Janeiro.

As of 1930, the accompaniment for sambas shifted from the rhythmic formulas associated with dance songs accompanied by choro groups to the multi-rhythmic *batucada*, produced by several layers of instruments, including *surdo*, *cuíca*, and *tamborim*. The tamborim is associated with a group of rhythmic figures that shine

Figure 1 Tresillo paradigm (Sandroni, 2012, p. 30)

in the percussion orchestra of *samba schools*, validating what Sandroni referred to as the "Estacio paradigm," as it debuted at the parades that started in Estácio, a working-class neighborhood in Rio de Janeiro, during carnival. A little more complex in its combination of double and triple values, the second type of accompaniment creates a kind of asymmetrical and additive rhythmic formula or guideline, in an uneven relationship as compared to European metrics.

Sandroni found the "countermetric" pattern of the latter style included in the melodies of the second halves of more modern sambas, based on his listening and review of the repertoire recorded by Francisco Alves (1898–1952). In this case, the "Estacio paradigm" (Figure 2) or the tamborim beat guideline appears in the melodic division (musical poetic scansion) that Alves, also known as the "Voice King," learned from his companionship with samba circle players.

Another interpretation of the rhythmic structure of modern urban samba was proposed by arranger and professor Roberto Gnattali in one of his Brazilian popular music classes, as quoted by Dilmar Miranda (2022, p. 298) in his study on carnivalization at the turn of the twentieth century in Rio de Janeiro. There were two instrumental articulations that boosted the evolution of samba schools dancing and singing in the streets: the *surdo de marcação*, with the strong pulse on the second beat of the measure, and the anticipation of the following measure articulated by the tamborim (Figure 3); both help to break the metric predictability of the binary measure. From this multi-rhythmic mesh "results a feeling of emptiness, of something suspended, luring the body to occupy it." Quoting sociologist Muniz Sodré (1998) in his classic study of samba as "the owner of the body," Miranda explains how these displacements lead to filling the beat with bodily movement.

2.2.2 Samba, a Symbol of the Nation

In addition to the musical changes that began to take place in the late 1920s, there was a political shift with the Vargas Era, when music and communication media played a significant role. As mentioned before, Vargas's political project was to concentrate political power under his command using the concept of

A   mi-nha vi - da é bo - a

Figure 2 Estácio paradigm (Sandroni, 2012, p. 207) – verse 5 from *Se você jurar* (Ismael Silva, Nilton Bastos e Francisco Alves, 1931) – Odeon 10747. Orquestra Copacabana. https://discografiabrasileira.com.br/fonograma/26222/se-voce-jurar

Figure 3 Rhythmic pattern of urban samba, emphasizing the anticipation note and the beat of the surdo in the second beat of the measure. Adapted from Miranda, 2022, p. 298 with small corrections thanks to Prof. Gnattali

a single "nation," the "Brazilian nation," as an alibi, as opposed to the fragmented local identities that underpinned the political legitimacy of the previous status quo. The post-1930 political effort taken was to forge a new idea of "national authenticity," building an imaginary based on a new standard rather than using symbols that already existed. This is why samba – and not traditional music, such as modinha – was elected the national symbol.

As Hermano Vianna mentions in his book *Mistério do Samba* (The Mistery of Samba) (2004), samba's transformation from a musical genre into Brazil's national music was not a sudden event, but the crowning of a centuries-old tradition of contacts between various social groups in an attempt to invent Brazilian popular identity and culture. As an emblematic example, Vianna mentions a "guitar night" centered around Gilberto Freyre, the anthropologist responsible for the positive interpretation of miscegenation in his book *Casa Grande e Senzala* (The Masters and The Slaves) (1933). Also attending the event were Donga, and Pixinguinha, an instrumentalist and composer of anthological choros, as well as an arranger, music producer, and conductor. In other words, the nationalization of samba was supported by a number of agents, including intellectuals (led by Gilberto Freyre) and musicians (the Pixinguinha group). Freyre and his fellows strove to turn miscegenation – until then considered the source of Brazilian "backwardness" – into its national pride, with samba then symbolizing the "vitality of Brazilian culture" (Vianna, 2004, p. 164).

Another important aspect in this process was the use of Rádio Nacional as the official radio network that could integrate the country and be a channel for informal education and propaganda. The radio's programming was quite eclectic. In the 1930s, it featured several affiliated musical ensembles, of jazz, tango, and what was then called "light salon music" (waltzes and operetta songs). The samba singers were accompanied by a regional group, generally made up of one or two guitars, *cavaquinho* (like an ukulele), tambourine, and one or two soloists (flute and/or clarinet). Half of the singers hired by Rádio Nacional performed "Brazilian music," while the other half sang "foreign music."

Radamés Gnattali (1906–1988), one of the maestros responsible for arranging and orchestrating at Rádio Nacional, began to change the Brazilian music "framework." He started arranging for small groups, trios, and quartets, and gradually enriched the orchestrations to the point that successful artists (such as Orlando Silva) demanded that type of orchestration for their records. Gnattali changed the general sound of interpretative performance of popular music in Brazil – changing the number of instruments in the orchestra and the function of certain instruments. Accepting percussionist Luciano Perrone's suggestion, he gave the brass a rhythmic function. Before this innovation, wind instruments only played melodic lines. This rhythmic pattern can be noted in "Aquarela do Brasil" (Brazilian watercolor), by Ary Barroso (1939).[12] By the mid-1940s, this type of orchestration had become a trademark of Brazilianness (Saroldi & Moreira, 1988, pp. 19–21). It should be noted, however, that making the brass move as a block can be perfectly related to the style of American big bands.

In the 1940s, with the introduction of *Um milhão de melodias* (One Million Melodies), a radio show sponsored by Coca-Cola, another type of orchestra was created: Orquestra Brasileira de Radamés Gnattali (Radamés Gnattali's Brazilian Orchestra). In each show broadcast, the orchestra's repertoire usually featured two new pieces, two "old" ones and three international hits. According to Gnattali himself (quoted by Saroldi & Moreira, 1988, pp. 30–31), Brazilian music should be centered around (two) acoustic guitars and a cavaquinho, like a jazz group was based on the piano (with drums, bass, and electric guitar).

Parallel to the growing development of Rádio Nacional orchestras, there were shows produced and hosted by characters such as Almirante (Admiral) (Henrique Foreis Domingues, 1908–1980), who was in charge, over a seven-year period, of nine shows with a certain musical nationalism as a backdrop. Just as Catulo da Paixão Cearense published collections of traditional music, Almirante played an important role in the transition of music from oral social memory to written social memory, producing radio shows and building an archive containing everything from sheet music to letters from the audience, later added to Museu da Imagem e do Som do Rio de Janeiro (MIS-RJ, Rio de Janeiro Museum of Image and Sound). Those included the show *O Pessoal da Velha Guarda* (Old Guard group), hosted and produced by Almirante between 1947 and 1952, under the musical direction of Pixinguinha, playing for the

---

[12] See "Aquarela do Brasil", subtitled "Cena Brasileira", by Ary Barroso, with Francisco Alves and Radamés & Orquestra. https://discografiabrasileira.com.br/fonograma/36287/aquarela-do-brasil-i.

audience live interpretations of traditional songs from the Rio Antigo serenades – polkas, schottisches, waltzes, modinhas, choros – from the late nineteenth and early twentieth centuries (Paes, 2012).

The reason for reviving a pre-samba historical period, which at the time was
a popular genre associated with the already established nationalism, was a desire
for music not "tainted" by commerce and modernization, a constant concern of
nationalist sectors. Regardless of any ideological motivation, this show contributed to promoting choro nationally and even canonizing Pixinguinha's repertoire
and musical style (McCann, 2004, as quoted by Paes, 2012).

The discussion about the national and the foreign "invasion" has been
a deeply rooted element in the essays and statements by many musicians,
journalists, and Brazilian music enthusiasts. However, in terms of sound,
several musicians have or had no problem using "foreign" elements in their
music. Just think of the orchestrations by Pixinguinha and Radamés Gnattali,
who used "jazz" nuances in songs considered "authentically" Brazilian. While
discourse represents an ideological position, musical arrangement and performance reveal the ambiguities of everyday practice, in an "enigmatic relationship
between cosmopolitan and national elements" (Volpe, 2022).

2.2.3 Samba Exaltação *and* Samba de Breque

From a historical perspective, Paranhos (2021) reviews the performance of samba
songs from the 1930s onward, questioning their apparent adherence to the order
established by the policy introduced by the Estado Novo dictatorship. Relying on
its official censorship bureau, namely Departamento de Imprensa e Propaganda
(DIP, Department of Press and Propaganda), the government fostered the exalt-
ation of nationality, such as with the "Brasil!" samba song, which was recorded
and released shortly before the well-known "Aquarela do Brasil," one of the most
famous songs depicting the "Brazilian landscape," mentioned earlier.[13] The
introductions of both sambas are openly grandiloquent, quoting parts of well-
known songs and using rhythmic motifs on melodic instruments.[14]

Some samba songs, however, escaped government control, and feature male
figures as protagonists complaining about the "martyrdom" of work and female

---

[13] "Brasil!" Singers: Francisco Alves and Dalva de Oliveira. Songwriters: Benedito Lacerda and
Aldo Cabral. [S. l.]: Columbia 55159, 1939. 78 rpm. https://discografiabrasileira.com.br/fono
grama/58486/brasil; "Aquarela do Brasil," Singers: Francisco Alves, accompanied by Radamés
Gnattali and His Orchestra. [s. l.]: Odeon 11768, 1939. 78 rpm. Matrix 6179. https://discogra
fiabrasileira.com.br/fonograma/36287/aquarela-do-brasil-i.

[14] The opening of "Brasil!" quotes the initial motif of the opera *O Guarany* overture, coincidentally
used in the opening of the government radio show *A hora do Brasil* (The Hour of Brazil), created
in 1935 during the Getúlio Vargas administration and still broadcast to date, although no longer
featuring Carlos Gomes's piece.

figures who love the night life. The hints of insubordination are, however, quite subtle, often appearing in performances and/or arrangements. For example, nothing in the lyrics or sheet music of songs like "O amor regenera o malandro" (Love Mends Hustlers), by Sebastião Figueiredo, as performed by Joel and Gaúcho, suggests the subversion of the original content that says that a "mended" man must work hard to receive a woman's affection. The insubordination appears in the "break" introduced only in the recorded album with the phrase "Que Horror!" (How Awful!). That is, the singers Joel and Gaúcho introduce, "in the manner of Bakhtin," a second voice in the apparently complimentary commentary on having a job.[15]

2.2.4 Bolero *and* Samba-Canção

While the intelligentsia and even some figures in the musical world were concerned with national identity–related issues, music was received by a large part of the population who tended to ignore the political dimension popular music was gaining. Research conducted on the aesthetics of popular music in Montes Claros, a medium-sized city in the north of Minas Gerais state, noted that in the 1940s and 1950s the local middle class danced to boleros, foxtrots, and waltzes, as well as to samba songs in local clubs (Carvalho, 1991). Both in Montes Claros and everywhere in the Brazilian territory with radio coverage, there was a large inflow of Latin American music in those decades. It was the pinnacle of rumbas, mambos, cha-chas, and especially boleros (Carvalho, 1991).

Bolero originated in Cuba at the end of the nineteenth century as a binary song accompanied by a rhythmic pattern known as the Cuban *cinquillo*, with two binary measures, the first with the five notes that name the pattern (eighth note-sixteenth note-eighth note), the second with four same-length notes (eighth notes) (Figure 4a). Bolero arrived in Brazil via Mexico, containing a bongo pattern (a *rulo*) that accentuates the second beat in a quaternary measure (Figure 4b). An emblematic example of this is the first bolero written in Brazil, that is, "Sob a máscara de veludo" (Under the Velvet Mask) (Alcir Pires Vermelho and David Nasser), with orchestral arrangement by Radamés Gnattali and interpretation by Francisco Alves (Carvalho, 1991, p. 82).[16]

Throughout the 1950s, bolero and samba-canção began to merge. In fact, it is perfectly possible to use the same instrumental accompaniment pattern for both

---

[15] "O amor regenera o malandro." Singers: Joel and Gaúcho. Songwriter: Sebastião Figueiredo. [S. l.]: Columbia 55211, 1940. 78 rpm. https://discografiabrasileira.com.br/fonograma/59053/o-amor-regenera-o-malandro.

[16] Columbia 55210, 1940. Available at *Discografia Brasileira*: https://discografiabrasileira.com.br/fonograma/59048/sob-a-mascara-de-veludo. The presence of several fragments referring to Brazilian, American, and Cuban music is to be noted.

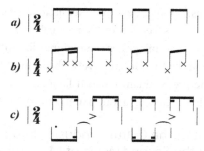

Figure 4 (a) The *cinquillo* Cubano, (b) bolero conga drum pattern, and (c) *samba-canção* / bossa nova backbone (adapted from Carvalho, 1991, p. 82).

genres. Although samba-canção, like samba, highlights the attacks of each beat, it accentuates the second half of the measure. (Figure 4c). As already mentioned, the forward momentum is there, as yet implicit – the second note in the characteristic cell sounds stronger than the first note simply because it is longer. The similar pattern that removes the emphasis on the attack of the first beat of the measure, as this occurs both in the Cuban cinquillo and in the pattern derived from bolero, as well as in the characteristic Andrade syncopation, facilitates the rhythmic integration of the genres (pp. 82–83).

Resuming the discussion about nationalist modernism, one can note the ambiguous relationship between local traditions and foreign repercussions. As we have already mentioned, the radio shows hosted by Almirante displayed a nationalist rhetoric despite the use of American musical genres. The same type of prejudice seems to apply to bolero. An emblematic example of this is the production of Lupicínio Rodrigues (1914–1974), which reached its peak around 1952, in a transitional phase prior to the "bossa nova revolution," and was considered a production of "*bolerized* and unqualified samba-canção" songs (Campos, 1974). In other words, bolero was an unappreciated musical genre due to its "foreign" connections, even though it was Latin American and closer to home (Ulhôa, 2010). The interesting thing is that all those appreciative analyses refer to the instrumental arrangement of the accompaniment that could emphasize local or foreign qualities. Mário de Andrade (1989, p. 348) listened to samba-canção phonograms in the 1930s accompanied by a traditional choro ensemble and mentioned that this musical genre offshoot would be the "final nationalization of modinha."

No one knows what the mentor of musical nationalism would say about the version of "Vingança" (Revenge), a classic by Lupicínio Rodrigues performed by Linda Batista in 1951, accompanied by an ensemble including piano, violin, double bass, and drums.[17] Regardless of either nationalist or modernist ideologies, in terms of sound, this version of "Vingança" – being at the same time samba and romantic music – integrates the two matrices of "Brazilian music," namely lundu and modinha, while creatively absorbing "foreign music" (the bolero), as well as the predominant musical language in American music. In other words, we are finally talking about popular music in Brazil.

2.3 Development of the Cultural Industry in Brazil, 1950–1980 and the Second Wave of Modernism

2.3.1 Quiet Nights of Quiet Stars: Bossa Nova, TV, and Consumer Society

Nowadays taken as synonymous with Brazilian popular music, bossa nova emerged amid several controversies, of an aesthetic, cultural, and even political nature, and peaked between 1958 and 1962 in Rio de Janeiro (Gava, 2002; Torres, 2015, p. 37). Marked by the impetus of the aesthetic modernization Brazilian arts underwent in the late 1950s, musicians like Antônio Carlos "Tom" Jobim, Vinícius de Moraes, João Gilberto, Carlos Lyra, Roberto Menescal, Elis Regina, Baden Powell, and others proposed some "modernization" of local popular music through the dialogue with contemporary music genres and styles, whether avant-garde music or postwar jazz. This aesthetic trend was in line with the political zeitgeist of the period: the postcolonialist movement sustained that peripheral countries in industrial capitalism should demand sovereignty through economic development, proposing an alternative to both American capitalism and Soviet communism. Bossa nova beginnings were in tandem with a period of growth driven by the industrialization of the national economy, especially during President Juscelino Kubitschek (JK) de Oliveira's administration (1955–1960). The "ideology of development" meant a strong belief in the nation's capacity to stand out in the world for its own, based on its own culture, its own singularity (Cardoso, 1978). The construction of the new federal capital, Brasília, led by urban planner Lúcio Costa and architect Oscar Niemeyer, seemed to materialize the "birth" of a new nation that imposed itself on the world order in a sophisticated and sovereign manner. Built from scratch, the city incorporated all the values that underpinned the modernist movement in architecture (Underwood, 2002), being a major material and cultural achievement of the then so-called "third world."

Regarding music, in the early 1950s, there were many vocal groups in Rio, such as Os Namorados, and numerous bars with live music in the neighborhoods of Copacabana and Ipanema, where artists such as Johnny Alf and Leny

---

[17] See https://discografiabrasileira.com.br/fonograma/78754/vinganca.

Andrade performed (Nestrovski, 2013; Torres, 2015). In the mid-1950s, two groups led musical innovations: on the one hand, songwriters such as Tom Jobim, Newton Mendonça, and Vinicius de Moraes were more involved with record companies and less with playing in bars; on the other hand, the group with Ronaldo Bôscoli, Nara Leão, Roberto Menescal, and Carlos Lyra was very present at university cultural centers (Castro, 2001).

The already well-established high-fidelity (hi-fi) recording technology and the rapid increase in the number of radios in Brazilian households allowed the emergence of cozy songs with a light vocal style and subtle instrumentation. This went well with lyrics with a colloquial and unpretentious style, different from the collective and noisy environments of auditoriums, so common at the time, and from the bolero and samba-canção songs, typical of radio stations, with which some young people did not identify (Torres, 2015). It no longer took a grand voice to reach the listeners, and the large band formations were replaced with vocals and guitar formations, with the guitar being an instrument that musically suited the intimate profile then sought.

This format was often used in performances by a single person, as was the case with João Gilberto (1931–2019), whose 1959 *Chega de Saudade* (No More Blues) "is considered the debut album of bossa nova" (Gomes, 2017, p. 41), leading Gilberto to be considered the genre paradigm. The appropriations of elements from classical music and jazz, as well as the "disengagement from love disagreements and melodramatic content" of bolero and samba-canção songs, are its main hallmarks (Gomes, 2017, p. 41).

On the guitar, Gilberto simplified the so-called *batucada do samba* (samba percussion jam) – the thumb was responsible for the regular catchphrases (which refer to the surdo, displacing it from the initial strong beat of the measure) and the other fingers for the irregularity of the tamborim (Garcia, 1999). Added to harmonic extensions, chromaticisms, pedal notes, and "long sequences of varied chords" (Gava, 2002, p. 240), as well as to the style of sentimental singers such as Mário Reis and Orlando Silva (Dunn, 2001, p. 28), these elements represented an amalgamation of Brazilian and American musical aspects. Bricolage, which was characteristic of the "samba jazz" from previous years (Gomes, 2010), was being left behind.

The rapport between the United States and Brazil was not without reason: with the end of the Second World War and the adoption of the US good neighbor policy, "the dissemination and consumption of symbolic American goods in Brazil," and some penetration of Brazilian symbols such as samba, and bossa nova in the United States intensified (Gomes, 2017, p. 35). The onset of the consumer society in Brazil marked the 1960s, when the market for goods such as automobiles and television sets was consolidated. As a new parameter of well-being and social status, the American way of life took over advertisements and the streets. Television quickly advertised products such as guitar and rock'n'roll (Garson, 2015). The boost in culture included promoting jazz performances, broadcasting radio shows, and advertising records on the music market (Saraiva, 2007). Significant names in the emergence of bossa nova such as Johnny Alf (1929–2010), João Donato (1934–2023), and Fafá Lemos (1921– 2004), were, for example, regulars at the Sinatra-Farney Fan Club, which played mostly American music (Castro, 2008). While the "elegant complexity" of jazz had already been foreshadowed in Pixinguinha's work decades earlier and consolidated in Radamés Gnattali's arrangements for the radio, it was now fully evident in bossa nova.

All of this led to criticism that *bossanovistas* (bossa nova musicians) were alienated from national culture and seemed to contradict the role of "major Brazilian musical genre" that bossa nova sought to occupy.[18] The fundamental pillar supporting the underlying commentary was, in fact, the idea that a modern country also generated modern music. At that time, much of what was considered regional or national in Brazil began to carry the connotation of "outdated" (Torres, 2015, p. 32). Conversely, the term "bossa nova" started to be used to express connotations of "modern, new, young, or interesting," even outside the music realm (Torres, 2015, p. 44). It is no coincidence that Kubitschek earned the nickname "bossa nova president," a label that was consolidated in the satirical song written by composer and comedian Juca Chaves (1938–2023), released in 1960 by the RGE-Brasil record label. This modernization process reduced the frequent use of instruments such as the accordion, incorporated melodic improvisation practices into songs, and gave samba songs from the 1930s and 1940s new harmonizations, also disseminating an alphanumeric notation system for instrumental accompaniment, previously not much used in Brazil (Chediak, 1986, p. 3).

Although bossa nova was packaged for the cultural goods market through albums and radio stations, it became one of the highest symbols of sophistication for local cultural critics. It was music made and consumed by a fraction of the local, young, and urban elite interested in the promise of modernity. Accordingly, the genre proved to have the ideal constituents to introduce new technologies for reproducing sounds to wealthier audiences. Conversely, such new technologies also gave bossa nova a certain aura of modernity, through the *new* reproduction technology, turning it into an object of desire for this high-income audience (De Marchi, 2016).

---

[18] In a famous article from 1966, José Ramos Tinhorão considered that BN was, in fact, a Brazilian form of jazz and represented a capitulation of true national culture to the cultural imperialism of the United States.

In addition to being an aesthetic landmark, bossa nova was also a vector of transformation for the music industry in Brazil, where television emerged already playing an essential role in this promise of modernity. In their initial phase, television shows were adapted forms of radio shows, with music as an essential element. Soon after this experimentation period of television language, two types of shows stood out: those specializing in specific musical categories (samba, bossa nova, international music, etc.) and those inspired by the success of the San Remo festival (Italy) with competitions among new songs, the so-called *song festivals*. Both show models were tried out by private TV stations.

TV Record, one of the first television stations in the country, decided to invest in music shows to attract the postwar youth. For those who listened to bossa nova and popular songs, there was *O Fino da Bossa* (The Best of Bossa), co-hosted by crooners Jair Rodrigues and Elis Regina, and for those interested in rock'n'roll, the there was a Sunday show called *Jovem Guarda* (literally, Young Guard; also, New School, in contrast to Old School).[19] Radio had already established a partnership with the music industry. The main radio stations had their own cast of musicians, arrangers, and singers, and TV stations only had to import radio music artists from radio to television to attract their audience with them.

In relation to records, it was with bossa nova that the LP format – a proposition consistent with the promise of modernity of new records and new high-fidelity players – was consolidated in the Brazilian market, although new technologies for reproducing sounds were adopted a little more slowly in the country. Bossa nova album covers were a milestone in this association between new Brazilian music and the new technology for reproducing sounds, as they began to feature the faces of young singers, using a graphic art style borrowed from advertising for the photos (Laus, 1998). Once again, the innovative pulse of the album *Chega de Saudade*, released in 1959 by João Gilberto, stands out: its cover distinctly features the singer's face surrounded by stylized letters with his name. Visual sophistication reached a new level with the records put out by the Elenco record label (1963–1984), whose black-and-white covers were signed by graphic artist César Villela.

Bossa nova was not the only movement of musical renewal during that period. However, by finding a meeting point between the samba of previous decades and international elements, the genre ensured its position as a national symbol to be advertised by the government. Musically, its promise of

---

[19] TV Record also created a television show dedicated to the hits of the radio era for older audiences used to radio singers. Despite its traditionalist profile, the show was titled *Bossaudade* (Bossa and longing). Television managed to imprint its feeling of modernity even to the nostalgia of times gone by, by switching the word "nova" (new) in "bossa nova" for "saudade" (longing) in "Bossaudade."

modernity based on a reinterpretation of Brazilian cultural traditions allowed it to be a reference for structuring the postwar artistic arena and, as a result, it had government support to travel the country and abroad under three administrations, namely, those of presidents Juscelino Kubitschek, Jânio Quadros, and João Goulart (Dunn, 2001, p. 29). In the United States, especially after the iconic concert at Carnegie Hall in 1962, bossa nova took over the imagery of Brazil, previously dedicated to samba, and began to significantly make its name as a paradigm in the so-called "Latin jazz." In its first two years, "Garota de Ipanema" (The Girl from Ipanema) was re-recorded on Brazilian and American soil more than forty times, also by renowned singers (Castro, 2008, pp. 314–315).

According to Augusto de Campos (1974, pp. 269–270), this was when Brazilian music stopped exporting the raw material of exoticism – as was the case with Carmen Miranda, who had to record caricatures of herself for the American movie industry – and began to export finished products from its creative industry. Jobim imposed his original repertoire in the United States (considering the large number of songs he had in the Real Book) and João Gilberto sang in Portuguese without translating his lyrics or changing his singing style, showcasing how bossa nova managed to consolidate itself as a successful internationalization project (Dunn, 2001).

2.3.2 The 1964 Coup D'état and the Dark Times of the Military Dictatorship

The development of popular music during that period cannot be dissociated from the political context that gave it a unique trajectory: the military dictatorship, which lasted from 1964 to 1985.

Despite the country's hope in its economy, the period was one of serious political tension (Dreifuss, 1981; Fernandes, 1975; Ferreira & Castro Gomes, 2016; Reis, 2014). The economic industrialization project that had been implemented by Getúlio Vargas since 1930 implied gradual wins in employment-related rights for the labor movement, which built up resistance from local business groups. The sovereign policy that underpinned the industrialization agenda caused resistance among military groups aligned with America's foreign policy. As demands for more democracy and social justice advanced in Brazilian society, conservative groups began to fear the outbreak of a *communist revolution*. Soon, they began to conspire against the advancement of democracy in Brazil.

Political instability reached its peak during the government of developmentalist João B. M. Goulart, known as "Jango," who took over the presidency in 1961. Its foreign policy was not aligned with that of the United States and its domestic policy on industrialization and social justice was considered a fully communist agenda by conservative political groups (*Jango*, 1984). On April 1, 1964, the Armed Forces carried out yet another coup d'état.

This kick-started brutal political repression, which included the suppression of political parties and unions, as well as the arrest and murder of political and social leaders. The preeminent civilians in the coup (liberal-conservative politicians and businesspeople) expected that the military would simply "clear the terrain," that is, "get rid" of labor party politicians (Vargas supporters) and communists – with the withdrawal of political rights, as well as extradition and murder – and then hand the power over to them. Among the military, however, there was no consensus on what to do after the coup d'état: whether to hand power over to professional politicians or to extend the military government. This scenario was not just a "backdrop." Rather, it defined the direction of music in Brazil over the coming years.

2.3.3 The Iê-Iê-Iê (Yeah-Yeah-Yeah) of Jovem Guarda

In this context, bossa nova was seen even more as the "guardian of national culture" (Dunn, 2001, p. 58) with the rise of jovem guarda, a select group of rock artists who had enormous commercial success as of 1963. Erasmo Carlos (1941–2022), Wanderléa (1944–), and especially Roberto Carlos (1941–) were the exponents of the so-called iê-iê-iê (yeah-yeah-yeah), an expression derived from the chorus of the Beatles song "She Loves You," which clearly stated the artists' main aesthetic reference and was used pejoratively by critics. Just like the English band, jovem guarda artists easily amassed large audiences and sparked the phenomena of "fans" and of the so-called "youth culture" in the country, promoting the production of films with soundtracks featuring iê-iê- iê songs. The three singers hosted and performed on the television show titled *Jovem Guarda*, which originated the label for this aesthetic.

The show was first broadcast in 1965, resulting from the combination of three factors, namely TV Record's need to fill its Sunday afternoon programming, which had been emptied in August of that year by the ban on live broadcasts of soccer matches; the decision of a publicist (Carlito Maia), partner at the Magaldi, Maia & Prosperi (MM&P) PR firm, to create and explore popular consumer idols; and the availability on the market of a young, talented, and ambitious singer with a career on the rise. This was when, on the one hand, shows began to emerge in a format that could in fact be considered for TV (Ribeiro, Sacramento & Roxo, 2010) and, on the other hand, popular music began to undergo an aesthetic and generational renewal, which made it easier for broadcasters to contact young artists who could cost less for companies and could renew the music industry through television.

Bearing all the costs of the project, the producer then hired the singer-hosts –
Roberto, Erasmo, and Wanderléa – of the show, bought television time, and set up
a strong advertising strategy, coining and registering terms and expressions that
were owned by the agency. Given the success of this venture, these terms and
expressions were leased to serve as brands for various commercial products
(Severiano, 2013). The success of the trio caused several singers and bands in
the same style to emerge, several of which performed as guests on the television
show. And the "passing fad" of Portuguese versions of international rock songs
(a common practice in the 1950s) gave way to a *musical movement* with original
songs.

With long hair and colorful looks, the iê-iê-iê artists contrasted with the sober
look of the bossa nova singers. In the bands, the guitar, bass, and drums
prevailed, along with the keyboard and a lively singing style, typical of 1960s
international rock, all of which supported lyrics that talked about positive
subjects. Jovem guarda did not sing about problems or difficulties. Their clear-
cut adaptation of American musical references, as well as the optimistic tone of
the lyrics, made them a target of strong nationalist criticism, which accused
them of being inauthentic and politically alienated. Even though the romantic
ballads of jovem guarda were rooted in nineteenth-century Brazilian modinhas
(Dunn, 2001, p. 58), it was the typical rock elements in "Splish Splash" and
"O Calhambeque" (Road Hog), by Roberto Carlos, that stood out. The close-
ness with the United States in the previous decade interested the Brazilian
government – now a military dictatorship – in a different way and encountered
even more resistance from part of the Brazilian population.

With a view to tapping into the political mobilization then generated by the
debate on music and politics in Brazil, TV Record began to encourage the hosts of
the two shows (*O Fino da Bossa* and *Jovem Guarda*) to spark a certain antagonism between their audiences. In fact, both the jovem guarda artists and those
connected to bossa nova and samba not only knew each other but were personal
friends and even partners in new compositions. Writing in the 1960s and 1970s,
Augusto de Campos considered that the issue involving foreign market subservi-
ence had been settled, even when referring to the most pop music of the time, the
jovem guarda. However, from TV Record's perspective, the antagonism could be
positively tapped, as the dispute between the two poles could lead to further –
using anachronistic language – *engagement* by fans with the shows. The battles
generated countless news and controversies exploited by the sensationalist media.

For intellectuals influenced by Marxist-leaning theories of the time, jovem
guarda was the greatest expression of capitalist alienation imposed on Brazilian
youth: its lyrics seemed to be part of an infantilization of listening (which
originated the pejorative iê-iê-iê label, in contrast with the sophisticated

argumentation of bossa nova lyrics), and the movies produced featuring the television show stars seemed to be nothing more than a compliment to the consumer society. Above all, the use of electric guitars was disturbing, as it was seen as a symbol of cultural imperialism: the use of electric musical instruments indicated that Brazilian culture capitulated to the modernity imported from capitalist metropolises, being a threat to some *authentic popular culture*.

2.3.4 The Era of Song Festivals

The success of the *Jovem Guarda* show – with its use of the lexicon and looks from the counterculture and electric musical instruments – created a certain antagonism with the political engagement of what was then called "popular music" and leftist cultural critics. The consolidated intellectual discussion about cultural imperialism (which in a way reflected the ideological and political conflict between developmentalists/communists and liberals) gained new material expressions. Now the dispute between acoustic and electric guitars was conditional upon the new means of communication of that moment, that is, the television. Amid ideological tensions brought about by the Cold War, this discussion, which might have seemed minor, became the platform for broader and more stressful political clashes.

As of 1965, the format of song festivals gained prominence. At that point, bossa nova and jovem guarda began to share the spotlight with the protest songs sung at the festivals that emerged after the civil-military dictatorship was established in the country. Organized by television stations, the festivals were extremely appealing musical competition events held at auditoriums, which also attracted the attention of major record companies. The so-called "Era of Festivals" was relatively short (1960–1972). It reached its peak between 1965 and 1969, but, like bossa nova, it had a great impact on aesthetic and political issues in the country and launched musicians who are still relevant today (Napolitano, 2001, 2010). Televised major song festivals gave rise to names such as Caetano Veloso (1942–), Chico Buarque de Hollanda, and Gilberto Gil (1942–), who shared the same stages with musicians already known for their connection with bossa nova, such as Elis Regina and Nara Leão (1942–1989), or with samba, such as Elza Soares (1930–2022) and Jair Rodrigues (1939–2014).

The first attempt at a song festival had been produced half a decade earlier, in 1960, with the *I Festa da Música Popular Brasileira* (1st Brazilian Popular Music Festival), a joint effort between TV Record and newspaper *Última Hora* (Homem de Mello, 2003). From this experience, competing stations also began to produce their own festivals, whose reverberation in the press attracted new composers and singers, turning television into the dynamic core of the music industry at that period. According to Marcos Napolitano (2010), festivals began to develop a truly television language (and no longer one imitative of radio) and to expand the artists' audiences, since people watched the festivals not so much for their musical genre, but for the disputes between songs, the public response, the comments of cultural critics, and gossip newspaper columns.

From a musical point of view, the songs introduced at the festivals had attributes that were familiar to the audiences, as they used elements from already well-established genres, such as *marchinha* (in "A Banda," by Chico Buarque), samba-canção (in "Roda Viva," also by Chico Buarque), and *moda de viola* (in "Disparada," by Geraldo Vandré and Théo de Barros). The vocals prevail in resistance songs, harmonized in a way that highlights the sung lyrics. Unlike the internationalization desired by bossa nova and the aesthetic renewal proposed by jovem guarda (both optimistic), the songs at the festivals reaffirmed the national cultural roots, in line with the country's musical traditions, and prioritized topics involving the serious political and social context at that time. (Freire & Augusto, 2014). This generation of songwriters from university festivals and concerts had aims similar to those of the *nova trova cubana* and the Latin American new song movement. It was then that an acronym emerged and quickly took over: MPB. The term "Brazilian Popular Music" reflected discussions about Brazilianness and summarized different expressions then in use: protest music, festival songs, politically engaged music, Modern Brazilian Popular Music (or Brazilian Modern Popular Music) (Vilarino, 2006, p. 19). There was tension between jovem guarda and bossa nova audiences (considered "alienated") and MPB audiences (considered "engaged"). The peak of this tension was on July 17, 1967, when artists linked to the second group organized a public protest against the use of electric guitars in Brazilian music, which became known as the "march against electric guitars" (Guimarães, 2014). The march against electric guitars itself was supported by the Record Group (Homem de Mello, 2003; Napolitano, 2010), considering that two of the main protest leaders were Elis Regina and Jair Rodrigues, the hosts of *O Fino da Bossa* show.

Similar to what happened to bossa nova and jovem guarda, the split between the world of bossa nova and MPB was not definite either, as noted in the partnership of Tom Jobim and Chico Buarque in "Sabiá" (Thrush). However, leaving aside long instrumental passages and valuing more singable melodic contours, the songs put lyrics at the forefront as a channel of resistance to the authoritarian advances of the military dictatorship. The festivals featured songs whose lyrics had to be previously submitted to censorship by the Federal Police, which could prohibit their performance or demand changes to the songs for them to be performed.

The songs, especially Buarque's songs, addressed periods, places, people, and everyday events that were not clearly stated, which also facilitated listeners to relate to the things and feelings sung. In the words of Vilarino (2006, p. 64), "the character in Chico Buarque's lyrics is collective." Listening to these songs without information about the Brazilian social context at the time "would make it difficult to assign them with the character of protest for which they became known" (Freire & Augusto, 2014, p. 228). In "Apesar de Você" (In Spite of You), the subject is grammatically indeterminate, but socially explicit: "Hoje você é quem manda, falou, tá falado, não tem discussão, não . . ." (Today you're in charge, you told me once, you've told me twice, end of discussion, yeah). At that time of political hardening, ideas imbued with a "revolutionary" feeling guided the political practice and artistic production of leftist sectors and permeated protest songs released in festivals (Napolitano, 2001; Ridenti, 2000).

The songs did not necessarily introduce great aesthetic or literary innovations, but they were able to accurately channel the feelings and criticisms of repressed society. What ensured its special relevance in society and attention from those in positions of power was mainly its project of going beyond the "role of entertainment to become an instrument of political awareness and, if possible, of taking power and social transformation" (Freire & Augusto, 2014, p. 223). "Pra não dizer que não falei das flores" (Not to Say I Didn't Speak of Flowers), by Geraldo Vandré, is the ideal example of these characteristics, and become a call for an armed combat to overthrow the regime.[20]

Thus, a second generation of composers and singers emerged. They proposed music based on the recovery of the so-called *Brazilian roots*, that is, of popular musical traditions.[21] With a certain air of late romanticism, these musicians promoted an aesthetic that emphasized the *national* element (in the sense of musical traditions originating from African, indigenous, and "sertanejo" cultures) and the *popular* element (from the practices of rural and urban populations) but read through modern music. These artists sought to create some *national-popular* art that could reflect a future for the Brazilian people: the *Brazilian nation* was a goal to be achieved. Such political momentum is imprinted on the very label given to this aesthetic – *Brazilian Popular Music* – whose reference to *popular* involves a notion that has nothing to do with the number of records sold or, even, the representation of the fascist concept of *people's community* (*Volksgemeinschaft*) (Chapoutot, 2022), but to the project of creating some Brazilian *new man*. Given its focus on key ideas such as *popular culture* and *national sovereignty* in the face of cultural influences from the United States, MPB – translated in protest songs at festivals – satisfied the desires of the left wingers in the ideological spectrum of Brazilian politics.

---

[20] The song took on several meanings, and its motto "quem sabe faz a hora" (those who know take action) was appropriated as political propaganda by the right wingers (Paranhos, 2014).

[21] Reference to the book *Raízes do Brasil* (Roots of Brazil), published in 1936 by sociologist and historian Sérgio Buarque de Hollanda.

2.3.5 Tropicália *and the Reinterpretation of International Pop Culture through the Lenses of Brazilian Popular Culture and Modernism*

Festivals were also essential for tropicália, a challenging and irreverent musical movement that emerged in 1967 and was also covered in the MPB umbrella term. Tropicália sought to rethink, by using songs, the notion of Brazilianness and "the transition from an exotic and timeless Brazil to a country of large urban centers" (Elias, 2015, p. 43), having, in parallel, a desire for internationalization. The movement's starting point was the 3rd Brazilian Popular Music Festival, held by TV Record in 1967, when Caetano Veloso (along with the Argentine rock group Beat Boys) and Gilberto Gil performed the songs "Alegria, Alegria" (Joy, Joy) and "Domingo no Parque" (Sunday in the Park), respectively. The instrumentation of "Alegria, Alegria" already summarized what was to come: orchestral instruments together with electric guitars and *berimbaus*.

While bossa nova represented a drive toward the modernization of harmonic sound, of instrumentation, and of the rhythmic aspects of how it is conducted, Tropicália sought to feed on everything that was happening – locally, nationally, and globally – to renew the arrangements, textures, harmony, and song lyrics. In order to adopt Oswald de Andrade's anthropophagous attitude and bring it to the field of music, the production model was concerned with originality and artistic elaboration.

The result of anthropophagy was summarized in the seminal *Tropicália ou Panis et Circensis* (Tropicália or Panis et Circensis), an album released in 1968. The album brought together Caetano Veloso, Gal Costa, Gilberto Gil, Tom Zé (1936–), and the three musicians from the band Os Mutantes (The Mutants), that is, Arnaldo Baptista (1948–), Sérgio Dias (1950–), and Rita Lee (1947–2023). In addition, José Carlos Capinam (1941–), Nara Leão and Torquato Neto (1944–1972) also participated in the album, while Rogério Duprat (1932–2006) was responsible for the arrangements. Combining music and concrete poetry, samba, orchestral instruments, rock, verses in Portuguese, Spanish and Latin, electric guitars and synthesizers, Batman, *ciranda*, and percussion of all types, the songs in the album seemed to ignore the borders between music genres and cultures. Unlike protest songs and bossa nova songs, "that music did not seem national, nor did it reproduce foreign models" (Elias, 2015, p. 39).

"Batmacumba," a voodoo-rock in the words of Charles Perrone (1985), added the superhero character Batman to the gesture of "beating" the drums in the style performed at sessions of Afro-Brazilian religions (bat' *macumba*). The traditional hybridizes with the modern (iê-iê) in opposition to the interjection "oba," identified by Béhague (1973) as an expression of rejoicing, but which also refers to the healing orisha Obalúayé. Tropicália reversed the relationship of national popular music – in this case, no longer "macumba for tourists" but "batmacumba for futurists" (Campos, 1974).

This represented a different way of thinking about Brazil as compared to how the protest songs did. The lyrics of protest songs addressed the political situation directly, while the music sounded traditional. Gilberto Gil and Caetano Veloso, however, were interested in reinterpreting Brazilianness also by formally and aesthetically exploring sounds, language, and visual aspects. The outfits were not well-behaved; rather, they were colorful and flashy. In self-criticism of MPB (Zan, 2001, p. 114), the tropicalist project required an expansion of the national imagery (Elias, 2015). Indifferent to a vision of Brazil centered on fauna, flora, and folklore covered in green and yellow, the *tropicalists* expressed the growing Brazilian cosmopolitanism, which was reflected in music through the choice of topics for the lyrics, the addition of rhythms of religious traditions, complex textures, and diverse instrumentation. Tropicália deepened the disruption created by bossa nova for the "codes of musical conventions" (Campos, 1974).

The march against the guitar, which seemed to Veloso an act of ideological intolerance, ended up leading to an aesthetic reformulation of the songs in MPB, which began to include not only the electric guitar but also countless references – either domestic or foreign. The commercial interest that galvanized the aesthetic and ideological dispute on television shows had decisive and unintended consequences for music. After tropicália, MPB songwriters included various genres into their repertoire, not only of other Brazilian regional sources (such as *baião*, xote, and *xaxado*) as happened in the 1950s, but also foreign genres (such as Jamaican reggae). The use of electric guitars by tropicália was a political decision toward the sovereign renewal of Brazilian traditions and not toward a submissive position to international imperialism. Pop music was, in this case, the input for some (post)modern Brazilian music that combined whatever was at hand. Thus, tropicalismo, through rock in the 1960s, broke the essential link between "Brazilian popular music" and samba, and managed to place itself as a member of this lineage, paving the way for rock with local characteristics and for MPB in the coming decades, when in fact the acronym "MPB" was repurposed as a musical genre.

Censorship was often followed by the arrest of musicians. The most dramatic case was the arrest of Caetano Veloso and Gilberto Gil in 1968. That was the year that had the most festivals, but also the year the regime became more intense, and, according to Homem de Mello (2003, p. 334), the year when festivals lost stamina. Based on false allegations of carrying marijuana, the two musicians were sent to a barracks in the suburbs of Rio de Janeiro, where they were tortured for fifty-four days. After being released, they both went into exile in Europe. The event made it clear to the artistic community that political repression also targeted the arts and that – to quote an important MPB song – nothing will be as it was, henceforward (*Nada será como antes*, Milton Nascimento and Ronaldo Bastos, 1972). Arrests and torture became frequent, creating a widespread feeling of insecurity (Freire & Augusto, 2014, p. 222). Even though many artists found brilliant strategies to circumvent censorship, the repressive apparatus hindered the arts and constrained the artistic creativity of the period in an incalculable way.

2.3.6 The Resurgence of the Military Dictatorship in 1968 and the Effects on Music in Brazil

It was only in 1968, after four years of repressed rights, that the military decided what to do in power. Instead of relaying power to professional politicians, they decided to extend the military government, when more radical groups within the Armed Forces became government leaders and implemented Institutional Act No. 5 (AI-5) on December 13, 1968. After that, political and ideological repression deepened even further. This was the onset of one of the most brutal moments in Brazilian politics, in which censorship, arbitrary arrests, torture, and systematic murders became instruments for managing daily life.

This political context decisively affected Brazilian popular music. In its first phase, the repression imposed by the military focused on political institutions (parties, unions, social movements) and individuals (politicians and party activists, as well as military personnel ideologically aligned with democratic forces). The arts were somewhat forsaken, since the military understood that *culture* did not matter. This was the opportunity for new Brazilian popular music to develop autonomously (Napolitano, 2001). The absence of systematic repression against the arts led bossa nova and MPB artists to continuously take part in demonstrations criticizing the military dictatorship. As political institutions were being disassembled, popular music played on radio and television, and records became one of the main platforms for messages opposing the regime (Napolitano, 2001). Names such as those of composers and performers Geraldo Vandré (1935–), Carlos Lyra (1933–2023), or Chico Buarque became important influencers in deploying youth against the dictatorship.

However, with the enactment of AI-5, the military also turned to the world of arts. The military intelligentsia realized that the arts were an important vector for building society's sensitivity. However, according to their worldview (*Weltanschauung*), the arts *indoctrinated* youth into the project of a communist revolution. So they deemed it important to stop this subversive movement (Ortiz, 1988). Therefore, it was necessary to ensure the dissemination of values that were dear to conservative groups, that is, the defense of capitalism and possessive individualism, as well as the values of the so-called traditional bourgeois and Christian family, a native moral category of conservative groups.

To carry out their plan of ideological containment, the military regime's policymakers implemented two supplementary strategies. On the one hand, the military established an official censorship apparatus. On the other hand, they encouraged the development of a professional mass culture production to oppose the national-popular culture of pro-left artists.

Deploying agencies such as the National Information Service (SNI) and the Department of Political and Social Order (DOPS), the military developed a sophisticated system of surveillance, censorship, and punishment, which not only prohibited the publication or staging of works but also ordered arrests and torture of artists.

Naturally, openly political topics were censored. But not only those. Moral-related topics were also on the censors' agenda. The openness to sexual experiences and the recreational use of drugs – causes supported by the counterculture that began to come out through tropicalism – also clashed with the values of the so-called *traditional family*. It is interesting to note that one of the genres that suffered the most censorship in this sense was the so-called brega music (Araújo, 2002). Its kitsch aesthetics and sentimental lyrics constantly alluded to passionate and even heterodox love relationships. Topics such as marital betrayal, prostitution, night life, and alcoholism, among other taboos, were not uncommon. The result was that brega music – seen as apolitical – was also the target of censorship. A paradigmatic case involved the song by composer and singer Odair José "Pare de tomar a pílula" (Stop Taking the Pill) (Odair José and Ana Maria), from 1973, which was about the contraceptive pill. In the lyrics, the singer asked his partner to stop taking the contraceptive pill so that she could get pregnant. At the time, the military governments had started a birth control campaign by giving away contraceptive pills to women from lower social classes. The song was thus considered *subversive* – to use the native jargon of the repressive apparatus – and was censored.

The black movement, which, at the time, was called Movimento Black Rio (Black Rio Movement),[22] was another notable case of political persecution. As of the mid-1970s, soul music started to arrive in Brazil on a more continuous basis, bringing together the political agenda of the American black power movement. Among black Brazilian youth, the black movement agenda and

---

[22] The label "Black Rio movement" came from an article published in 1976, by journalist Lena Frias in *Jornal do Brasil*, titled "Movimento Black Rio: o orgulho (importado) de ser negro" (Black Rio Movement: The (Imported) Pride of Being Black). The title Black Rio then started to be attributed to the cultural expressions of the Brazilian black movement.

aesthetics gained strength, paving the way for the so-called soul and funk *bailes* (parties or dances)[23] and for the use of pan-Africanist aesthetics (black power hair, traditional African clothes, slang translated from films and lyrics from the American black movement). For the government's repression apparatus, the Black Rio movement was at the convergence between political danger (concern for the establishment of a Black Panther Party cell in the country) and moral threat (the affirmation of a black identity that challenged the myth of racial democracy in Brazil[24]) (Peixoto & Sebadelhe, 2016). This was followed by arrests, lyrics being censored, and the degrading of several participants in this emerging music scene, from cultural producers to DJs.

2.3.7 The Economic Miracle of the Recording Industry

While it censored artists perceived as subversive, the dictatorship implemented a policy to support the development of the music industry. The word *industry* is decisive here. As the military intelligentsia saw it, the field of arts was controlled by *communists* who got organized through the different arts, from MPB musicians to Cinema Novo filmmakers. The solution to disassemble this "leftist plot" was to encourage mass culture produced by private companies that would introduce the public to consumer society. Setting the cultural industry and its *international-popular culture* against the national-popular culture seemed to be a strategic maneuver for the purpose of the so-called National Security against communism (Ortiz, 1988).

This led off to a number of measures aimed at boosting the production of *cultural assets*. Numerous incentives were given to the publishing, television, and advertising industries, as well as to the movie industry, for importing equipment, building cultural companies, and accessing credit to expand production, among other measures (Ortiz, 1988). It was not about a proclaimed *cultural policy* for the arts, but rather an *industrial policy* for culture.

As for music, the government granted every incentive possible for the expansion of the recording industry by supporting record companies. In

---

[23] At that time, the word "funk" referred to US funk. "Funk carioca" (Rio de Janeiro funk) would only take shape later.

[24] Throughout the nineteenth century, the idea that the so-called Brazilian *people* were inferior due to their miscegenation prevailed among Brazilian intellectuals. With *Casa Grande e Senzala* (The Masters and the Slaves), a book published in 1933 by anthropologist Gilberto Freyre (2003), the diagnosis was reversed: Brazil had the power of some new civilization thanks precisely to its miscegenation. According to Freyre's theory, there was a type of racial harmonization through sexual intercourse that placed the Brazilian people in parentheses in relation to the racist theory categories of the time: not white, black, or indigenous, but a mix of races. This type of thinking served as the basis for an argument – supported, above all, by the most conservative social strata – of *racial democracy*. When the Black Rio movement raised the agenda of the American black movement, it directly attacked the idea of racial democracy.

accordance with the industrialist policy of the military governments, lines of credit became available for importing musical and sound recording instruments, as well as for manufacturing record players and other sound reproduction devices. Specifically for the record companies, the military governments supported the campaign *Disco é Cultura* (Records Are Culture), a tax incentive policy for record production in Brazil to subsidize the recording of new Brazilian artists (Prestes Filho, 2005).

More important, however, was the enactment of a new copyright law, Law No. 5 988, of December 14, 1973. It introduced important changes in the record market regulation. One of its most decisive elements referred to the collective management of copyright. Brazil has the unique characteristic of having several entities collecting copyright rights.[25] The new law introduced a critical novelty: it established the agency that would have a monopoly on centralizing the collection and distribution of copyright royalties, namely, the Escritório Central de Arrecadação e Distribuição (ECAD, Central Collection and Distribution Office).[26]

The policies designed for the field of culture had significant results. In the case of the music industry, record companies were the most favored. Between 1967 and 1980, acquisitions of record players increased by 813% (Ortiz, 1988). This meant that, combined with the tax incentive for Brazilian music production, the revenue of recording companies increased by 1,375% between 1970 and 1976 (Ortiz, 1988). According to data from Associação Brasileira dos Produtores de Discos (ABPD, Brazilian Association of Record Producers), cited by Rita Morelli (2009, p. 86), the record market in the country grew by 7% in 1970, by 19% in 1971, and by 26% in the first half of 1972 alone. Between 1965 and 1972, according to the same source, sales growth in the segment was 400%. Finally, in 1979, Brazil became the sixth most profitable record market in the world, according to the IFPI.

The economic opportunities offered by a developing country motivated the arrival of a new wave of multinational record labels. From the 1970s onward, however, some companies actively fought for Brazilian market share: Warner, Elektra & Atlantic (WEA) in 1976, and Capitol Records in 1978, the year in which Polygram took over its former local partner, Companhia Brasileira de Discos Phonogram (Dias, 2000; Midani, 2008; Morelli, 2009; Vicente, 2014). As they began to operate in the country, they sought to sign the main names in the

---

[25] Unlike most other large music markets, Brazil experienced the phenomenon of the multiplication of collecting entities. See Morelli, 2009; Prestes Filho, 2005.

[26] In the first draft of the wording, ECAD was supposed to replace all collecting associations. However, the battle initiated by influential publishers resulted in the law being changed. The final version stated that ECAD should be managed by these same associations. This means that ECAD would be like an "association managed by associations" (Prestes Filho, 2005, p. 428).

national market. When Algerian-Brazilian music producer André Midani was its CEO, WEA signed the main MPB stars and became, in one fell swoop, one of the biggest record sellers in the market. Little by little, large multinational record companies took over the market share of small and medium-sized Brazilian record companies, which were forced to explore market niches, such as romantic/brega music, sertanejo, and soul music. This ended up creating a new market structure split into multinationals and Brazilian record companies.[27]

The presence and power of the multinational record companies caused discomfort among the most politically engaged artists. There were constant accusations of (1) misuse of funds obtained through tax incentives, (2) *Americanization* of the music produced in the country, and (3) surreptitious payments made by multinational record companies to have their artists' songs played more frequently in the media (payola). Unable to have their complaints heard by politicians, many artists realized that they could produce their works in a completely independent manner, that is, they financed the recording and distribution of their works. Famous for his complaints against major record companies, singer Tim Maia (1942–1998) released the two volumes of his 1975 album *Racional* (Rational) through Seroma, the label created by him. In 1977, pianist and composer Antônio Adolfo (1947–) released the album *Feito em Casa* (Homemade). In São Paulo, musicians from a new generation of MPB singers and songwriters – including, but not limited to, Arrigo Barnabé (1951–), Itamar Assumpção (1949–2003), Grupo Rumo, Língua de Trapo, and Premeditando o Breque – gathered around the movement known as Vanguarda Paulista (Sao Paulo Avant-Garde), and released their albums independently (Mário, 1986; Vaz, 1988). *Boca Livre*, the first album released by the vocal quartet Boca Livre in 1979, marked the great commercial success of this independent experience: the album managed to exceed 100,000 copies sold the year it was released.

Despite having been an important platform to introduce new artists or for the aesthetic maturity of already known artists, this first attempt at independent production began to decline throughout the 1980s. As a result, many artists ended up either signing with major record companies or developing their careers outside the musical mainstream, without consolidating the independent sector as a well-established segment in the domestic recording industry.

---

[27] Except for the then record label Som Livre, the recording arm of Grupo Globo media. In the 1970s, the record and publishing company was responsible for publishing and recording the songs that participated in song competitions. From the 1980s onward, the record company was in charge of releasing the soundtracks for the soap operas produced by Rede Globo (Globo TV). In 2022, Grupo Globo sold the company to Sony Music.

2.3.8 Para O Dia Nascer Feliz (For a New Happy Day): BRock from the 1980s

The 1980s were another period of intense and mixed feelings. On the one hand, the fight against the dictatorship obtained support from all sectors of the population, leading to the end of the military regime in 1985 and culminating in the proclamation of a new constitution in 1988. On the other hand, the military was successful in taking control of the democratization process according to its interests, frustrating advances proposed by social movements. Moreover, the crisis of its industrialist policy generated a deep economic depression, causing the period to be known as the *lost decade*.

In music, the period started off amid the uncertainties brought about by the global and local economic crisis. First, the oil crisis affected the supply of vinyl, making the plans for growth in record sales to be suddenly replaced by declining production. Additionally, soaring domestic inflation began to severely restrict the consumer market for cultural goods (Dias, 2000).

However, this was when a new generation of musicians influenced by punk rock and new wave emerged. While this generation seemed to represent a break from Brazilian music tradition (especially with the MPB aesthetics), it was marked by social criticism not so much through engaging lyrics, like in the 1960s, but by a demand for change in status quo. Faced with the need to renew their rosters to attract new consumers, major record companies began to sign these young artists. Bands like Blitz or Paralamas do Sucesso began to stand out on the radio, leading the way for other artists of the same generation. However, their commercial consolidation came with the first edition of the Rock in Rio festival,[28] held in the city of Rio de Janeiro in 1985. Businessman Roberto Medina managed to bring together big international stars, such as Queen, Iron Maiden, Ozzy Osbourne, Yes, Al Jarreau, James Taylor, and Rod Stewart, to play at an international festival. To open the concerts, the event's production team called on young artists of what was beginning to be labeled new Brazilian rock, or BRock (Dapieve, 1995).

The success of the festival consolidated these young artists as part of a new post-dictatorship generation. In particular, the chorus of the song "Pro dia nascer feliz" (For a New Happy Day), by the band Barão Vermelho, which says "Estamos, meu bem / Por um triz / Pro dia nascer feliz" (We are hanging on by a thread, baby, for a new happy day), sung in 1985, just before the power was handed over by the military to civilians, sounded like the announcement of new

---

[28] Originally, the Rock in Rio festival was supposed to have only one edition. However, given its commercial and iconic success, Roberto Medina sought to organize new editions, turning the festival into an annual event.

times. In fact, figures from the record industry showed that the music market began to recover as of 1985, still with vinyl records and cassette tapes (De Marchi, 2016).

The 1980s concluded a development cycle in the record industry with extraordinary modernization of its production structure and expansion of the consumer market, but at the cost of a strong market concentration in multinational record companies located in the Rio de Janeiro-São Paulo hub. This movement created the material conditions for diversifying musical genres produced by Brazilian musicians across market niches, although strongly split into mainstream music (MPB and, from the 1980s, BRock) and musical genres designed for less affluent classes (romantic music, sertanejo, and soul music). The 1990s would significantly change this scenario, with the rise of subalterns in the field of music.

3 Globalization and Musical Diversity

3.1 The New Republic and the Decentralization of Cultural Production 1990–2000

Throughout the 1980s, the brutality of political repression and growing inflation contributed to undermining the legitimacy of the military among different sectors of society. This expanded the spectrum of social forces that fought the dictatorship, allowing the formation of a broad political front. Its most important expression was the *Diretas Já* movement, which in 1984 demanded direct presidential elections. The movement took to the streets and became bigger. However, while still in power, the military managed to frustrate the demand for democracy. Faced with a legislative power aligned with the military, the majority of congressmen and senators opted for indirect elections to elect the then first president of the civil republic since 1964.

The country handed over by the military was in ruins: systemic corruption between the state bureaucracy and private capital, devastated political institutions, hyperinflation, foreign debt, economic stagnation, and, most importantly, the absence of a culture of democracy. The economic crisis was such that the political class that took power after the generals was unable to resume economic growth. Numerous economic plans were tried, without success.

At that point, economists and politicians with liberal thoughts – but of a new type – began to be noticed by the media. Mirroring the ideas and policies of Margaret Thatcher and Ronald Reagan, these agents advocated for a complete opening of the Brazilian economy to the globalized market, reducing the "size" of the State and encouraging competitive practices. Neoliberal ideologues stormed the stage and promised to save the economy.

This group of economists designed a new fiat currency, the Real, and with the introduction of a price index (which worked as a camouflaged and temporary dollarization of the Brazilian economy), they managed to curb inflation and somewhat stabilize the economy. By creating a currency that was practically worth the same as the dollar and radically opening the Brazilian market to imported products, family consumption increased rapidly after 1993, generating tremendous excitement among the middle class. The success of the so-called Real Plan would make the then Finance Secretary, sociologist Fernando Henrique Cardoso (FHC, a member of the Brazilian Social Democratic Party, PSDB), the *savior of the country* in the eyes of the media. In 1994, FHC won the presidential election against Luís Inácio Lula da Silva (Workers' Party, or PT in the Portuguese acronym) and implemented a neoliberal political agenda that included a policy of fiscal austerity, privatization of government-owned companies, immediate opening of the Brazilian market to international capital, and adoption of fiscal policies to attract international financial capital.

At the cultural level, that was when the idea of the nation-state began to become weaker, and local knowledge – or *glocal*, as unsuccessfully labeled at some point – was once again appreciated. Artists claimed access to the global market from their location, in their accent, exhorting their regional traditions. In the case of music, this was a very important window of opportunity for artists from outside the Rio de Janeiro-São Paulo hub. The most notable example is that of the band Chico Science & Nação Zumbi. Originally from the city of Recife, in the northeastern state of Pernambuco, these musicians sought to revive *maracatu*, a traditional musical genre, by mixing it with rock, pop, and electronic music.[29] Their second album, *Afrociberdelia* (1996, Sony Music Brasil), became a milestone in Brazilian pop music. Their career could have been even more glorious hadn't it been for the tragic death of its leader and composer, Francisco de Assis França, aka Chico Science, in a car accident between the cities of Recife and Olinda on February 2, 1997.

In Salvador da Bahia, local musicians developed a type of popular music that mixed Afro-Brazilian musical traditions with pop music, which came to be known as axé music. Artists such as *É o Tchan* and *Banda Eva* and its singer Ivete Sangalo were very successful outside of Bahia, even topping the charts in the Rio de Janeiro-São Paulo hub.

Even sertanejo, Brazil's country music – often seen in large urban centers as aesthetically inferior, naive, and even tacky or cheesy – began to adopt the sound and look of country music from the United States, revolutionizing the traditional

---

[29] The musical characteristics of the artists discussed here, as well as their relationship with the dispute between tradition and modernity, are further explored in Section 3.2, *Mass Popular Music*.

musical genre and turning it into pop music. This bold move made this musical genre one of the most commercially successful in the charts. As a matter of fact, the success of sertanejo artists (who no longer seemed to reflect almost anything from the old imagery of the *sertão*) indicated the power of agribusiness in the Brazilian economy vis-à-vis a consumer goods industry in complete decline.

Even in Rio de Janeiro and São Paulo, what began to attract attention was no longer the pop-rock music made by the children of a well-educated middle class, but the songs that echoed from the poorest and most excluded areas of the cities: from *periferias*, in the case of São Paulo, or *favelas*, in Rio de Janeiro. That was the time of the rise of rap from São Paulo and funk from Rio de Janeiro. These two genres originated from the Black Rio movement. In the 1980s, the so-called *bailes de música black* (black music parties or dances, which played soul music, R&B, funk) migrated from central urban areas to more distant neighborhoods (periferias) and more dangerous places to live (favelas), where most of the Afro-descendant population lived.

In São Paulo, the black movement was mostly influenced by New York rap. In Rio de Janeiro, personal relationships between local DJs and cultural inter-mediaries living in Miami (USA) made the so-called Miami Bass the main musical influence (Vianna, 1988). Although they shared the same political roots and the same cultural references, these genres evolved independently of one another, which led to important stylistic differences.

Given this scenario, the once cool pop-rock/post-punk from the 1980s seemed to have become *démodé*. Music in Brazil began to show a diversity that revealed the components of a new society (a) no longer restricted to the coast, having moved inland, (b) that became urban, but at the cost of brutal social inequality, (c) that began to listen to the demands for social recognition from different social groups (Afro-Brazilians, agribusiness rural residents, people from the Northeast, among others). Their struggle for recognition, to use the expression coined by Axel Honneth (1996), outlined the ideological and political clash that marked the country in the decades to follow.

3.1.1 The CD, the New Independent Artists and the Golden Age of the Record Sales

For the Brazilian music industry, the 1990s were a true rollercoaster. The decade began under the effects of a serious economic crisis. Between 1989 and 1990, for example, the total number of records sold went down from 76,686 million units to 45,225 million units (Dias, 2000). The year 1992 was even worse, with a significant decline of 31.48% in units sold and 29.98% in revenue reported by the main record companies. In view of the crisis, the major record companies adopted the business management model known as the lean model, as was already the case in economically developed countries.

This meant, above all, the outsourcing of productive functions. Accordingly, the companies started to sell assets (recording studios, design departments, and other functions that were previously performed internally by the company) and to fire long-term employees, from sound technicians to senior executives. Even the catalog management rules were revised. Traditional MPB or BRock stars, already aging, did not have their contracts renewed. The new executives of the major record companies began to seek out artists from musical genres that had more commercial appeal on the most popular radio stations. This A&R renewal favored musical genres such as *pagode* (a subgenre of samba originated in Rio de Janeiro in the late 1970s), axé music, and the new romantic sertanejo.

The most important measure of the period was the adoption of the digital disc, the Compact Disc (CD). While CDs were introduced in economically developed markets in the early 1980s, in Brazil, the new technology was delayed until the end of the decade (1986) and was actually adopted on an industrial scale only in the 1990s. The major record companies believed that the CD was a product that would require large financial disbursements on the part of consumers during one of the most serious economic crises in the country. Following the economic recovery driven by the Real Plan, the record companies realized that it was time to consolidate the CD in the market. After all, the Real Plan was based on completely opening the Brazilian market to imported products and the parity between the US dollar and the Brazilian real, which boosted consumerism among the middle strata of the population.

In order for the new media to be quickly embraced by consumers, it was decided that the production of vinyl records and cassette tapes should be dramatically reduced (Prestes Filho, 2005). This shock therapy made vinyl records more expensive while the new media had a standard price, which was the same as the international market price, that is, around US$15.00 (Vicente, 2014). Thus, while in 1987 the price of one CD was equivalent to the price of two LPs, in 1991 this ratio was reversed: one LP was now equivalent to two CDs. That year, the Brazilian music industry earned US$28.4 million from the sale of LPs, while the figure for CDs was as little as US$7.5 million. In 1994, the numbers were down to US$14.5 million for vinyl and up to US$40.2 million for digital discs (Prestes Filho, 2005).

The adoption of digital technologies by the formal music industry also led to changes in the relationship with informal sales, otherwise known as piracy. The parallel industry of unauthorized reproduction of sound recordings emerged with pirated cassette tapes in the 1970s. However, the record companies believed that this form of piracy was residual or even beneficial, since it introduced a lower-income audience to the consumption of some type of recorded music. At that time, pirated copies were mainly produced in Paraguay (a country that borders Brazil to the southwest), where copies were recorded and reproduced on a large scale. The units were purchased by Brazilian traders on the border between the countries and distributed to street vendors to sell them in the streets and street markets in the main Brazilian cities (Prestes Filho, 2005). This entire structure was about to change with the adoption of digital technologies by cultural industries (cinema, music, and, above all, electronic games). The need for large factories to copy large amounts of digital content meant that the production center for pirated copies moved to Asia (China and Vietnam, among other centers), where they began to be exported to several countries (Prestes Filho, 2005). From then on, it was Eastern and Brazilian traders who took over the business operation. The trade in pirated goods increased unprecedentedly.

The digitalization of sound recordings and music consumption also allowed the consolidation of independent production. As the major record labels got rid of parts of the production chain and fired artists and specialized employees, an opportunity opened up for the development of new independent record labels. Thus, a new generation of independent record labels emerged (De Marchi, 2006a; Vicente, 2014).

At first, these companies sought to gain market share that seemed unimportant from the perspective of the major record companies. Some focused on producing new artists from different musical genres. This was the case with Abril Music, DeckDiscs, or Trama. Others focused on recording famous artists who were not, however, interested in attaining the major companies' productivity goals. A notable case was Biscoito Fino, which specializes in MPB and Brazilian jazz. Little by little, the good practices adopted by these record companies also enabled them to compete with the big record companies on the charts, establishing themselves as part of the production structure of the recording industry. They were responsible for renewing the music scene, launching artists such as the rock singer Pitty (1977–), the band Los Hermanos, the sertanejo duo Bruno & Marrone, the new MPB singer Max de Castro (1972–), experimental musicians such as Otto, electronic music DJs such as DJ Marky Mark (1951–) and DJ Patife (1976–), the electronic forró band Falamansa, and romantic samba groups, such as ArtPopular.

Another important factor in the recovery of the recording industry was the debut of MTV Brasil in 1990. Grupo Abril media group signed off on a licensing of the MTV brand in the country, managing, however, the broadcaster's editorial policy. Having a television channel exclusively dedicated to the music industry – albeit limited to pay-television subscribers – allowed, in the first place, to break the monopoly that Rede Globo television had on the broadcast of record label artists and, secondly, to expand the visibility of artists from new independent record labels to a new generation of consumers. The channel remained one of the main showcases for the music industry until 2013.

The change in the recorded music market structure was decisive for record companies to recover their profits throughout the decade. In 1993, there was a 42.71% increase in unit sales and a 66.61% increase in revenue. This recovery trend was confirmed in 1994, during the Real Plan, when 63 million units were sold and revenue of US$782.5 million was reported. In 1995, there was a 12.69% increase in unit sales (71 million) and an 18.84% increase in revenue of major record labels (US$930 million). In 1996, the Brazilian record industry sold 99.8 million units and reported US$1,394.5 million in earnings, which brought it back to the position of sixth largest record music market in the world according to IFPI.

3.2 Mass Popular Music

In the internet age, musical practices are aterritorial, in a scenario that Ortiz (1988) would call international-popular.

The opening up of the country in political and commercial terms, combined with the fast migration to digital formats (initially CDs and then the internet), led several Brazilian regions to more quickly absorb music from other regions of the country and of the world. As in the 1960s, musicians were entangled in discussions involving "tradition-modernity," permeated by the "national-international" dichotomy on a massive scale. But, while the conflict was then channeled through televised festivals, in the 1990s this tension materialized in regional clashes, thanks to emerging digital technologies. They made traffic more agile and encouraged more diverse expressions, as it was no longer necessary for music novelties to go through large centers and then be rolled out to other regions.

Some genres that were split up and faced well-defined disputes over authenticity at that time include forró (in Ceará, Pernambuco, and Paraíba), samba (in São Paulo), *funk carioca* (in Rio de Janeiro), and sertanejo (in São Paulo, Minas Gerais, and Goiás). In the early 1990s, the mix of elements such as keyboards, drums, urban and romantic themes, amplification and dances aimed at young audiences inaugurated the so-called "electronic forró," which had the band Mastruz com Leite as one of its icons (Trotta, 2014). Other bands emerged at the same time – such as Cavalo de Pau, Mel com Terra and Banda Aquarius – and won a large audience with this new way of doing forró. These bands were quickly qualified by critics as an opposition to the so-called *forró pé de serra* (Santos, 2014), a direct heir to the traditional music of Jackson do Pandeiro

(1919–1982), Luiz Gonzaga (1912–1989), and Dominguinhos (1942–2013), which favored acoustic instruments (accordion, triangle, and zabumba) and sang about romance and the "old-fashioned" rural environment.

The deep market divide between electronic forró bands and forró pé de serra artists served as an argument for the split between musical quality and non-musical quality (Trotta, 2014, p. 18). This opposition was – and still is – seen as a discursive rivalry. In practice, however, there is a flow between the two styles, given that new artists often refer to the past, and already famous artists such as Alcymar Monteiro (1953–) and Assisão (1941–), involved in forró pé de serra, began to include instruments such as keyboard, brass, bass, and drums in their performances.

As was the case with forró, "the 1990s resembled a true era of extremes in the symbolic universe of samba" (Fernandes, 2011). At the end of the 1980s, *samba de pagode* from Rio de Janeiro – for example, by Zeca Pagodinho and Fundo de Quintal – lost share in record sales and radio plays. This paved the way for samba de pagode groups from the neighboring states of Minas Gerais and São Paulo at the beginning of the following decade (Araújo, 2000) to quickly establish their hegemony, especially in the periphery (D'Andrea, 2018).

Representatives of this emerging genre are Raça Negra, Só pra Contrariar, Soweto, and Katinguelê (Fernandes & Pulici, 2016, p. 135), groups comprising six or more men (women are rarely part of pagode samba groups). Musically, pagode began to add pop elements and instruments such as keyboard, electric bass, electric guitar, and saxophone, which began to be as important as (or more important than) traditional instruments such as banjo, *tantã* (tan-tan) and *repinique de mão*. Some pagode groups like ExaltaSamba, Molejo, and ArtPopular were structured in such a way that their members on stage had the same importance; that is, no particular component was in the spotlight, which alluded to the samba circle environment. On the other hand, in the case of the group Só Pra Contrariar, singer Alexandre Pires (1976–), who was its producer and owner, stood out. Live music performances became less improvised, with romantic topics prevailing in the lyrics of samba de pagode, which also con-ferred to it the name *pagode romantico* (in addition to *sambalanço*, *samba metal*, and *pagode paulista*). The groups began their careers in bars and small concert halls and, as they advanced professionally, they got rid of the look typically associated with bohemian nightlife and *malandragem* (trickery) to adopt an attitude of ostentatious designer clothes and jewelry (Araújo, 2000, pp. 111–112). The success of *pagode romantico* brought back samba artists who "excitedly called for the return of authenticity" at the end of the decade (Fernandes, 2011, p. 226). This movement did not happen in Rio de Janeiro, but in the city of São Paulo, where it gained support from local traditional "sambaists" who did not see themselves represented in the genre that was in evidence in the industry.

At the same time in Rio de Janeiro, an opposition between funk and *charme* was established. At that point, the so-called *melôs* – songs with lyrics in Portuguese, American rap samples, and the beat of Miami bass – prevailed in funk carioca. Funk gained many followers in the periphery of the city (Sá, 2007) and its hybrid nature led it to be considered "the first Brazilian genre of electronic dance music" (Palombini, 2009). The big release of the time was the album *Funk Brasil* by DJ Marlboro (1963–) and, although the entire scene was already referred to as "funk," many songs from this period show the word "rap" in their title, such as "Rap da Felicidade" (Cidinho & Doca) and "Rap do Silva" (MC Bob Rum). Funk was quickly associated with criminality and lewdness by the media and the intellectual elite (Bragança, 2017; Herschmann, 2000). At the same time, rhythm and blues from the United States gained ground in *bailes* (parties/dances) held in the suburbs of Rio, where the Viaduto de Madureira dance stands out to this day. Because it was slower and more melodious, which led to a slower and more sensual dance, Brazilian R&B gradually gained a name that was easier to assimilate, that is, charme (Miranda, 2019). "Rap da Diferença" (MCs Markinhos and Dollores) was notable precisely for opposing the two genres, seeking to associate charme with a culture of peace, party, and sensuality.

At that time, sertanejo had already added some elements of international music, such as the use of electric guitars from American country music and the synthesizers and melodic traits of international pop, which were then intertwined with the vocal style and classical formation of sertanejo duos from previous decades and the romantic themes of 1960s jovem guarda, and the ballads of the 1970s and 1980s (Ulhôa, 1999; Zan, 2001). The look of the genre was also greatly impacted by American imagery, from hair styles to the suede fringe shirts, as worn by the duo Chitãozinho & Xororó. This mix was referred to as *sertanejo romântico* (romantic sertanejo). Here, the two singers (who rarely played instruments during their performances) were still featured prominently on album covers and concert posters, but musically were always accompanied by their bands. Other prominent duos include Milionário & José Rico, Leandro & Leonardo, Zezé Di Camargo & Luciano, Rionegro & Solimões, Chrystian & Ralf, and João Paulo & Daniel. Although sertanejo is marked by duo formations, solo singers such as Roberta Miranda and Sérgio Reis have also played an important role in the history of the genre (Azevedo, 2022; Zan, 2001).

Opposing this more romantic and globalized branch of the sertanejo musical genre, there was a movement that focused on grassroots country music traditions (*música caipira*), with artists such as Almir Sater (1956–), Roberto Corrêa

(1957–), Renato Teixeira (1945–), Ivan Vilela (1962–), and Miltinho Edilberto (196?–) (Almeida, 2013). These artists' songs were still *modas de viola* sung and played by duos with acoustic instruments traditional to música caipira from the first half of the twentieth century. This repertoire also opens up to instrumental music, which highlights the accordion and *viola caipira*, an instrument that gradually gained more popularity in Brazil and was embraced by other musical genres throughout the country (Moraes, 2020).

But the 1990s were not just about disputes between the "traditional" and the "modern" in Brazil. The musical diversity, as well as the free circulation of songs made in other countries, can still be seen in the rising popularity of rap in Brazil (mainly established in the city of São Paulo), in the introduction of manguebeat in Recife, in axé music in Salvador, and lambada and *tecnobrega* in the state of Pará. These genres treat the duo "tradition-modernity" in their history more as partners than as opposing and conflicting views, being examples of the power of international musical circulation in music made in Brazil.

Racionais MCs, in São Paulo, were the main exponents of the rise of Brazilian cocorap in the early 1990s, with their main references being black music – already widespread in the São Paulo periphery, especially Tim Maia and Jorge Ben Jor (1939–) – and American rap. The band won over a significant audience by singing, in a direct and accusatory tone, about the conditions of young black and poor people from marginalized neighborhoods of the largest city in the country (D'Andrea, 2018). The rap sung by Racionais expresses the uncomfortable reality by putting together singing in an everyday speaking style (with little variation in pitch and at high speed) and percussion (equally dry, overshadowing the melodic and harmonic instruments). The use of a chorus no longer exists. It is the small rhythmic differences in singing, always related to the words sung, that create movement on the so-called "bases," repeated throughout long sections. Since the beginning of the Racionais' career, this candidness has transcended musical limits, translating topics such as drugs, police violence, and racism into youth awareness campaigns. Rap groups that emerged in other cities, such as Sistema Negro (in Campinas) and Planet Hemp (in Rio de Janeiro), are also known for adopting this tone of social accusation.

It was in Recife that manguebeat arose. It was a movement that managed to bring together a great musical variety in the early 1990s, mixing rap, electronic music, rock, and traditional genres such as coco, ciranda, maracatu, and embolada (Mendonça, 2019). In the music made by Chico Science & Nação Zumbi and by Mundo Livre S.A., considered icons of the genre, one can hear maracatu's typical instrument (*alfaia,* a Brazilian membranophone) and electric guitars in the style of Jimi Hendrix, along with critical lyrics written by Chico Science (1966–1997) and Fred Zero Quatro (1965–). The aesthetic diversity, which also extends to the music of Mestre Ambrósio, Devotos, and Faces do Subúrbio, contributed to promoting and giving new meaning to ancient expressions of Pernambuco culture. While in Recife the group Faces do Subúrbio declaims lyrics in the rhythm of embolada challenges over bases using tambourine percussion, in Rio de Janeiro MV Bill (1974–), the most well-known local rapper, records with samba musicians.

Moreover, the axé music production hub was established in the city of Salvador, Bahia state, in a true melting pot that put together *frevo*, reggae, *merengue*, forró, *samba duro*, samba-reggae, *ijexá* and typical rhythms of candomblé, pop-rock, *galope*, salsa, and lambada, among others (Castro, 2010; Pereira, 2010). This movement resulted from musical phenomena born in the 1970s, although the song "Fricote," sung by Luiz Caldas (1963–) in 1985, is often cited as the initial milestone in the renewal of the Bahian music market (Adão & Teixeira, 2020). Years before that, the *trios elétricos* (decorated trucks on top of which musicians play electrified instruments) of Dodô & Osmar and Moraes Moreira already mixed those elements (Pereira, 2010) and, parallel to them, *blocos de carnaval* and *afoxés* (groups of people dancing and partying together in "blocks") proliferated in Salvador. The latter included Ilê-Ayê (the first "Afro-block," an advocate of blackness and exclusive to afro-descendants), Filhos de Gandhy (afoxé that defends principles of non-violence and peace), and Olodum (derived from Ilê-Ayê, focused on community activism and with international perspectives). Closely related to cultural and religious expressions in Salvador, these groups made figures such as Carlinhos Brown, Daniela Mercury, and Margareth Menezes (Minister of Culture since 2023) popular among audiences.

The axé music of the 1990s – music sung and danced to at the big street carnival festivities in Salvador – brought together the pop instrumentation of electric guitars and double basses, keyboards, and winds with the great diversity of percussive instruments of Afro-American music. In Bahia, groups such as Chiclete com Banana, Banda Eva, and Banda Mel, and singers like Ivete Sangalo (1972–), then leaving Banda Eva and, once again, Daniela Mercury were successful, while the first group with a sequence of national hits was Gerasamba (later renamed É o Tchan). Although at that time axé did not establish itself in other traditional carnival festivities in Brazil, it gained a place in off-season carnivals, the so-called "micaretas." According to D'Andrea (2018), "for the first time in history, the establishment of Bahian dance music ... surpassed the sambas of Rio de Janeiro in importance and dissemination."

The international significance of the musicians involved in this afoxé and axé music scenario is also to be highlighted. Although the word "axé" is a greeting associated with Candomblé and Umbanda meaning positive energy, the expression "Axé Music" was coined by a journalist from the south of the country who mocked the international aspirations of these artists (Adão & Teixeira, 2020). This expression ended up catching on and became a marketing label. In the years that followed, these artists gained international recognition, with the most famous example being Olodum's featuring in recordings and performances by artists such as Paul Simon, Michael Jackson, and Tracy Chapman (Nunes, 1997).

In Belém, the dance tradition was *carimbó*, led by Verequete (1916–2009) and Pinduca (1937–). As an offshoot of carimbó, lambada emerged in the 1990s and became internationally famous. In the 2000s, the so-called tecnobrega appeared as a combination of melodramatic romantic music (brega) with *cumbia*, calypso, and merengue/bachata. Tecnobrega is produced with computers used as home recording studios, using software to produce songs used in gigantic multimedia parties ("equipment" parties), under the coordination of a DJ (such as DJ Gilmar, from the Rubi sound system) (Guerreiro do Amaral, 2014; Lemos & Castro, 2008). Another type of music in vogue in the city was *guitarrada*, made known by Mestre Vieira (1934–2018), in which cumbia, carimbó, and merengue solos are played on electric guitar. Breaking away from the idea of copying foreign genres, these songs combine local characteristics and external elements to the point of establishing themselves as new genres or subgenres. Accordingly, tecnobrega and lambada joined the list of genres that are recognized as participating in a flow of musical references that ignore national borders.

In this context, official commentary on diversity begins to take hold. In the next decade, according to 2003–2008 Minister of Culture Gilberto Gil, the important thing: "is to recognize difference as a value . . . musical syncretism that unites the tailcoat with the electric guitar, and the tambourine with the laptop, thus expressing both tradition and modernization" (Nicolau Netto, 2009, p. 166). From a cultural perspective, this is the commentary that introduces the twenty-first century, politically emphasizing multiculturalism and with the creation of the "Brazil" brand by the Ministry of Culture of the Lula administration.

3.3 Musical Kaleidoscope in the Twenty-First Century

3.3.1 The Creative Destruction of the Recording Industry

The outsourcing of productive functions in record companies reached a new level when new recording software applications that run on personal computers, the so-called Digital Audio Workstations (DAW), became accessible. Applications such as Pro-Tools, Cubase, or Logic, the several plug-ins that simulated sound effects, electronic instruments, and sample libraries created an media ecosystem for digital and portable sound production. As the digitalization of sound recordings advanced, the traditional jobs in record companies passed on to the music producers and artists themselves. The preproduction, production, and postproduction stages started to be carried out on PCs and the audios were recorded on CD-ROMs on the artists' own computers. This allowed for an increase in the number of so-called home studios, previously dedicated only to the preproduction of records. With the availability of DAWs, artists began to envision the possibility of doing without record companies, becoming completely independent.

The easier access to digital music recording also had an impact on consumption. The ability to connect CD recorders to PCs and the development of software for playing music in compact digital files represented a step as decisive as unexpected for the recording industry. Two phenomena deriving from this deserve attention.

On the one hand, the availability of this type of equipment allowed the illegal copying industry to become local, since local pirates no longer had to rely on importing records from the East. They could then buy a certain number of CD-ROM recorders and set up veritable cottage industries, in which they burned various copies of an official CD or DVD on their own computers to pass on to street vendors who would sell them on the streets informally. This expanded the scope of piracy. According to data provided by the former Brazilian Association of Record Producers (ABPD),[30] while the pirated content traded in 1997 was 3% of total record market sales, in 2002 this figure jumped to 59% (ABPD, 2004). On the other hand, the equipment made it possible for any user to transfer files from CDs to their HDs. In order to reduce the amount of data storage required, file compression software began to be used in licensed and free formats, that is, MPEG Audio Layer 3 or MP3. As files accumulated, more powerful software for organizing and playing music files began to be used, such as Winamp. Thus, the conditions to enable a revolution in the distribution of digital music were laid out (De Marchi, 2023).

Unhappy with the CD format, consumers migrated either to P2P or to the piracy market, creating a strong network effect. In Brazil, the result was devastating for the record industry. In fiscal year 2000, the former ABPD recorded sales of 94 million CDs and DVDs, or up 6.38% from the previous year. However, unit sales continuously declined from 2001 onward. Between 2000 and 2001, there was a sharp decrease of 23.4% in these numbers. Between 2002 and 2003,

---

[30] In a collection of articles on this topic organized by Oona Castro and Pedro Mizukami (2013), several authors raised doubts about the calculation methodology adopted by ABPD and equivalent associations for the film or IT industry. According to this argument, the associations' calculations were based on the number of CDs seized by the Brazilian police. As the number of CDs produced was high, the number estimated by the recording industry was impressive. However, there is no guarantee that all pirated CDs produced would actually be sold.

a significant decrease of 24.3% was experienced again. Between 2008 and 2009, the decrease was 17.89%, when 25.7 million discs were sold. A comparison of physical disc units sold in the years 2000 and 2009 showed a decrease of some 72.66% (De Marchi, 2016).

Baffled by the collapse of their business, both major and independent record companies were paralyzed, dedicating their time solely to the crusade against piracy. The sharp drop in the perceived value of recorded music paved the way for a profound transformation in the music economy. Live concerts were immediately elevated to the status of this industry's main business, being the only way to generate financial returns for artists (Herschmann, 2010). Concerts began to be seen as unique experiences of sociability, entertainment, and appreciation of company brands, which potentially could be explored commercially.

The apathy of record companies opened up an opportunity for musicians to become independent artists (De Marchi, 2016). As the sales of records had declined dramatically, new artists began to realize that a contractual relationship with a record label had become disadvantageous. Thus, many musicians started their own businesses[31] and began to (1) finance the recording of their albums to (2) distribute them free of charge over the internet, especially through their websites where (3) they could sell promotional products (T-shirts, buttons, key chains, mugs, as well as LPs, CDs, and DVDs in deluxe formats). This aimed at turning their own fan bases into transmitters of their works by sharing them over the internet, to produce a network effect that would attract more and more consumers to live concerts. The experience of independent artists managed to be somewhat successful amid the acute crisis in the music industry, as was the case with bands such as O Teatro Mágico, Móveis Coloniais de Acaju, or ForFun.

An important variation of this commercial strategy was developed by music producers and artists who dealt with an audience that did not have full access to broadband internet. In those cases, the artists decided to join pirate traders to promote their works. According to Ronaldo Lemos and Oona Castro (2008), the tecnobrega scene in the state of Pará, northern Brazil, evolved from a business model in which artists recorded their songs in home studios and passed their CDs and DVDs on to street vendors to sell them at low prices on the city streets. The proceeds from the sale of records (the price was around US$2.00) went to the street vendors. The artists were mostly interested in creating a network effect that would bring a larger audience to their concerts, which ultimately were their core business. This open business style (Lemos & Castro, 2008) obtained good results,

---

[31] This was done in the form of Individual Microenterprises (MEI), which had been introduced into Brazilian labor legislation in 2008 and allowed professionals without a formal employment agreement to formalize their informal commercial activities, with legal support and legal certainty.

helping to introduce artists from Pará to the national music scene, with the most notable case being that of singer Gaby Amarantos (1978–).

Finally, in view of the record companies' inability to innovate, Brazilian start-ups emerged to introduce the first technological solutions for digital music distribution. Still in the early 2000s, companies such as iMusica, Trevo Digital, or Trama Virtual began to experiment with possible ways of selling digital music or accessing music file streams, suggesting positive solutions for the recording industry (De Marchi, 2016).

Regardless of errors in business management or the quality of their techno-logical solutions, these companies created a digital music market even before any business model was established on an international level (iTunes). For a number of reasons, these start-up entities ended up not consolidating the digital market, which eventually led to global digital platforms.[32]

3.3.2 Aesthetic Fragmentation and Identity Politics

The context of creative destruction of the music economy set out the conditions for a diversity of musical experiences. The new generation of artists that emerged from the 2000s onward seemed not to care about the rules imposed by the market to differentiate musical genres or the temporality of the record market. As record companies and radio stations were no longer able to operate as intermediaries (gatekeepers) in the music market, artists began to experiment with sounds as well as business models. Given the stupor of the mainstream music market, numerous niches were being consolidated through independent artists and small independent recording companies.

The so-called "evolutionary line" of Brazilian popular music seemed to have broken in favor of a kaleidoscope of musical genres. While artists such as DJ Marky Mark (1975–), Soul Slinger, Nego Moçambique, and Bossa Cuca Nova produced electronic music in line with what was happening in European avant-garde clubs (house, drum'n'bass, techno, trip-hop, and acid jazz, among others), young musicians relived the tradition of choro, samba, frevo, maracatu, and even blocos de carnaval. Additionally, following the path led by Chico Science & Nação Zumbi, new artists continued to mix traditional musical genres and

---

[32] According to De Marchi (2023), some of the reasons that explain the misfortune of this generation of Brazilian start-ups are circumstantial, such as the lack of trust in these small IT companies by music industry players and the technical problems arising from their technological solutions. Furthermore, there were structural factors, such as the absence of smartphones and their app economy (which made it difficult for users to access the catalogs of digital companies) and the forthcoming potential for international digital platforms entering the Brazilian market (which means that players preferred to wait for a more opportune moment to invest in the digital market). Finally, at the time, there was not any support from the Brazilian government to encourage the digital recording industry in Brazil.

pop music: tecnobrega and guitarrada indicated the new way of mixing carimbó with electric guitars and/or electronic beats.

As the struggle on the part of social movements for the recognition of historically subaltern groups gained ground on the public agenda, artists who built their careers around supporting political causes – through their sound, lyrics, and, above all, their bodies – began to emerge. These are artists who do not hesitate to publicly take a stand in favor of feminist, LGBTQIA+, and black movement agendas, or, also, the rights of indigenous peoples. More than making engaged music as in the 1960s, it is about the artists using the image of their bodies to promote a revolution in the microphysics of power: through video clips that go viral on YouTube or TikTok, they build their careers through performances (Cunha, Soares & Oliveira, 2016; Soares, 2014), affirming themselves as women, as non-binary, as people of African descent, and/or as members of indigenous nations.

Transgender singers such as Pabllo Vittar (1993–), Liniker (1995–), Lin da Quebrada (1990–), or Ventura Profana (1993–) stand out not only for the qualities of their lyrics and music, but also for illustrating the way of life of LGBTQIA+ groups. Songwriters and singers such as Luedji Luna (1987–), Marina Iris (1984–), and Rachel Reis (1998–) built their careers writing songs about their condition as black women from the periphery (Gumes, Garson & Argôlo, 2023). Songwriter and lyricist Katú Mirim (1986–) stands out for bringing together songs from the Boe Bororo people, of whom she is a descendent, and rap and electronic music to address topics such as her sexual orientation or the massacre of original peoples. Along the same lines, the group Brô MCs, whose members come from the Guarani and Kaiowá peoples, raps in the Guarani language to denounce the crimes that white people systematically commit against their people.

These artists use the aesthetics of contemporary pop music to convey messages that address their struggle for social recognition. This may bring about a discussion of a post-musical genre era (Vargas & Carvalho, 2021), which means that music starts to be completed by performances that politicize everyday existence.

3.3.3 The "Platformization" of the Music Industry

The 2010s were a turning point in the digitalization of the music market. After more than a decade of frustrated digital distribution experiences, global digital platforms began to operate in Brazil. This consolidated the digital music market. There are two milestones in this phase: the agreement between YouTube and the Central Copyright Collection and Distribution Office (ECAD), and the agreement between Apple Inc. and the collecting entity União Brasileira de Editoras de Música (UBEM, Brazilian Union of Music Publishers) (De Marchi, 2023).

Although YouTube had been serving Brazilian users since 2007, it was only in 2010 that Google reached an agreement with ECAD and created a formula for the company to pay for videos protected by copyright. In 2011, it was Apple's turn to sign an agreement with UBEM (a copyright collecting entity formed by the main music publishers) to pay copyright royalties in order to operate as Apple's one-stop-shop for iTunes Stores. Although these agreements did not fully eliminate the problem of legal uncertainty for investments in Brazil, they at least established a channel for dialogue between copyright holders and international digital platforms.

Soon, a whole new layer of global digital gatekeepers began to operate in Brazil. Initially, the country received international digital distributors such as The Orchard (USA) and Believe Digital (UK), which began to mediate access to digital platforms by record companies and artists. Then, streaming services entered the country, such as Rdio (USA), Napster (USA), and Deezer (France), seeking to amass users before the entry of Spotify (UK), the most prominent international player at that time.

Contrary to what had happened with Brazilian start-ups, local content producers immediately joined their system. This changed the course of the digital music market. From the start, digital music stores took the place of Brazilian stores. As soon as iTunes started up its operations, stores like iMusica and Mercado da Música stopped serving end consumers. Competition extended to the lucrative cell phone market. While in the 2000s iMusica virtually monopolized this profitable niche of the digital market, in the following decade cell phone carriers began to enter into agreements with international streaming services. Oi signed with Rdio, TIM partnered with Deezer, and Vivo offered the services of a renewed Napster. As a result of this loss in market share, in 2014 the phone carrier Claro (a subsidiary of the Mexican company America Móvil) bought the shares of iMusica (Ideiasnet), turning it into Claro Música. Brazilian companies had to explore market niches, including web radios or streaming services dedicated to certain segments, such as Sua Música streaming service, which specialized in the Brazilian northeastern music industry.

Even independent artists joined the platform economy through digital distributors. While giving away their music on physical media for free to attract audiences was a tactic considered appropriate in the past, the possibility of uploading songs to iTunes or Deezer seemed like an alternative strategy that could generate some financial return for the artists. The distribution of songs via websites was gradually replaced by digital distributors hired to upload the artists' music to new digital platforms.

In 2014, Spotify finally began operations in Brazil. It soon became the leading music streaming service. Tidal, Apple Music, Amazon Music, among others, followed in its footsteps, consolidating streaming services as a means of accessing the flow of digital music. According to data from Pro-Música (new ABPD brand since 2016), streaming began to gain prominence in 2012, when it started to account for 25.3% of the digital segment, against 21.3% for paid downloads. In 2015, for the first time, revenue from the digital segment exceeded the sales of physical discs by 60.6% of the total market. In 2017, streaming accounted for 55.1% of the digital segment. In 2021, streaming contributed 85.6% to the music industry's total revenue in the country (Pro-Música Brasil, 2022).

As digital platforms developed into a music business model, artists began to plan their careers according to the rules adopted by these companies; that is, they would no longer release albums, but singles that were strategically inserted into editorial playlists of the main streaming services in order to attract plays and views.

This was also when record companies and record labels emerged on platforms like SoundCloud and YouTube, which, since then, have supported the production of musicians and groups in the Brazilian peripheries. With the ability to reach millions of people throughout the country, São Paulo producers such as GR6 and KondZilla introduced funk artists and hits that took over parties and celebrations, including names like MC Nego Blue (1990–), MC Léo da Baixada (1992–), and MC João (1991–). Relying on high-quality productions, the songs combine timbres of funk carioca and American pop with lyrics about bailes (dances) and parties, displaying some degree of ostentation, a word that would name the subgenre that emerged in the 2010s, the so-called *funk ostentação* (ostentatious funk). The success of such ventures does not go by unnoticed: these are the largest Brazilian music channels on YouTube, with Kondzilla being the largest Brazilian channel in all categories.

One of the artists who best understood the new model by which the music industry was operating was the pop singer Anitta (1993–). The artist began her career in funk carioca and gradually transformed her music into American pop with Latin American influences. Her career has been marked more by the release of singles than albums and by video clip performances that generate controversy on social media. This stirs her fan base, who make their clips and tweets go viral to protect their muse from attacks by online haters. The engagement of fans (and haters) leads the streaming services algorithms to identify her as the most relevant to the general public, further circulating the singer's work and image. On March 25, 2022, her lead single "Envolver" (NEO/WEA Latina), sung in Spanish, reached no. 1 on the daily Spotify Global Chart.

Coda

In mid-2023, an advertisement from a German car manufacturer caused commotion among the Brazilian audience when it used Deep Fake, an Artificial Intelligence (AI) technique, to reunite singer Elis Regina, who passed away in 1982, with her daughter Maria Rita (1977–), also a singer. When Elis Regina died, Maria Rita was very young and, therefore, had had only a brief relationship with her mother. They both performed the protest song written by Belchior (1946–2017) – a singer and songwriter who died in 2017 – "Como nossos pais" (Like Our Parents), released in 1976. The advertisement raised discussions about ethics and advertising and, of course, copyright. Although these controversies were important, little was mentioned about the fact that the advertisement introduced to the music industry in Brazil the production of songs made using AI – an innovation that promises to subvert the concept of "creativity" and the practices adopted for production and consumption of recorded music (De Marchi, 2023). AI shuffled the past, present, and future of Brazilian popular music in a new way, opening up other possibilities for popular music going forward.

Throughout this Element, we aimed to recover the history of popular music in Brazil in its conceptual, sociological, and musicological dimensions. We discussed what was defined as "Brazilian music" and "popular" among the local intellectual class. We refer to the development of musical genres to the different stages of the country's social and economic development. We sought to present an overview, albeit brief, of the musical genres that developed in the country, also mentioning some of the most notable artists and songs. This is surely not a comprehensive list. We only hope that such mentions serve as a guide for future research on popular music in Brazil.

More importantly than mentioning the names of artists and hit songs in different times, our purpose was to offer an overview of popular music in Brazil, since when folk music became "popular music," as early as the middle of the nineteenth century, to the musical kaleidoscope that characterizes the music industry in the twenty-first century. The objective was to reveal bridges between MPB and maxixe, between bossa nova and samba-canção, between BRock and bossa nova, between Chico Science and frevo or, even, between Anitta and Carmen Miranda – leading the way to understanding the bridge between Elis Regina and AI.

Finally, we hope to have presented to readers unfamiliar with popular music and its industry in Brazil a little about its history and the diversity of artists and musical genres in the country.

References

ABPD. (2004). *Mercado brasileiro de música 2003*. Rio de Janeiro: ABPD.

Adão, A. B. & Teixeira, G. de J. (2020). Música e discurso. *Revista Crioula*, 26, 11–22.

Adorno, T. W. (2001). Free time. In Adorno, T. W., eds., *The Culture Industry*. London: Free Time, Routledge, pp. 187–197.

Almeida, R. T. (2013). "Viola de dez cordas," Master Thesis, Universidade Federal de Minas Gerais, Belo Horizonte.

Alonso, G. (2015). *Cowboys do Asfalto*, Rio de Janeiro: Civilização Brasileira.

Andrade, M. (1964). *Modinhas Imperiais*, São Paulo: Livraria Martins Editora.

Andrade, M. (1989). *Dicionário Musical Brasileiro*. Belo Horizonte: Editora Itatiaia.

Andrade, M. (2020). *Ensaio sobre a música brasileira*, São Paulo: Editora da Universidade de São Paulo (EDUSP).

Andrade, O. (2017). *Manifesto antropofágico e outros textos*, São Paulo: Companhia das Letras.

Aragão, P. (2015). Choro manuscript collections of the 19th and early 20th centuries. In Ulhôa, M. T., Azevedo, C. and Trotta, F., eds., *Made in Brazil*. New York: Routledge, pp. 30–42.

Araújo, C. A. A. (2000). "Balançando o Brasil," Master Thesis, Universidade Federal de Minas Gerais, Belo Horizonte.

Araújo, P. C. (2002). *Eu não sou cachorro, não*, Rio de Janeiro: Record.

Augusto, A. J. (2011). *A questão Cavalier*, Rio de Janeiro: Folha Seca.

Azevedo, A. V. F. de. (2022). "O Acontecimento do 'feminejo'," Master Thesis, Universidade do Vale do Rio dos Sinos, São Leopoldo.

Baia, Silvano Fernandes. (2010). "A historiografia da música popular no Brasil (1971–1999)," PhD dissertation, Universidade de São Paulo, São Paulo.

Barbosa, M. (2013). *História da comunicação no Brasil*, Petrópolis: Editora Vozes.

Bernardes, R. (2006). José Maurício Nunes Garcia e a Real Capela de D. João VI no Rio de Janeiro. In Ministério das Relações Exteriores, *Textos do Brasil*, Ministério, Brasília, pp. 40–45.

Béhague, G. (1973). Bossa & Bossas. *Ethnomusicology*, 17(2), 209–233.

Bolaño, C. (2007). *Qual a lógica das políticas de comunicação no Brasil?* São Paulo: Paulus.

Bragança, J. da S. (2017). "Porque o funk está preso na gaiola," Master Thesis, Universidade Federal Rural do Rio de Janeiro, Rio de Janeiro.

Burkart, P. & Mccourt, T. (2006). *Digital Music Wars*, Lanham: Rowman & Littlefield.

Calabre, L. (2004). *A era do rádio*, Rio de Janeiro: Jorge Zahar Editor.

Campos, A. de. (1974). *Balanço da bossa e outras bossas*, São Paulo: Perspectiva.

Cardoso, M. L. (1978). *Ideologia do desenvolvimento no Brasil*, Rio de Janeiro: Paz e Terra.

Cardoso, A. (2008). *A música na corte de D. João VI*, São Paulo: Martins Fontes.

Carvalho, M. de U. (1991). "'Música popular' in Montes Claros, Minas Gerais, Brazil," PhD dissertation, Cornell University, Ithaca.

Carvalho, M. de U. (1995). Tupi or not Tupi MPB. In Matta, R. Da and Hess, D., eds., *The Brazilian Puzzle*. New York: Columbia University Press, pp. 159–179.

Castro, A. A. (2010). Axé music. *Per Musi*, 22, 203–217.

Castro, R. (2001). *A onda que se ergueu no mar*, São Paulo: Companhia das Letras.

Castro, R. (2008). *Chega de Saudade*, São Paulo: Companhia das Letras.

Castro, O. & Mizukami, P. (org.). (2013). *Brasil pirata, Brasil original*, Rio de Janeiro: Folio Digital: Letra e Imagem.

Cazes, H. (1999). *Choro*, São Paulo: Editora, p. 34.

Chapoutot, J. (2022). *A revolução cultural nazista*, Rio de Janeiro: Leonardo Da Vinci.

Chediak, A. (1986). *Harmonia e Improvisação*, Rio de Janeiro: Lumiar.

Costa-Lima Neto, L. (2018). *Entre o lundu, a ária e a aleluia*, Rio de Janeiro: Folha Seca.

Costa Neto, R. J. M. (2015). "E tem choro no Maranhão?" Master Thesis, Universidade Federal de Minas Gerais, Belo Horizonte.

Cravo Albin, R. (superv.). (2021). *Dicionário Cravo Albin de Música Popular Brasileira*, Rio de Janeiro: Instituto Cultural Cravo Albin.

Crowl, H. (2006). A música no Brasil colonial anterior à chegada da corte de D. João VI. In Ministério das Relações Exteriores, *Textos do Brasil*, Ministério, Brasília, 12, pp. 22–28.

Cunha, S. E., Soares, T. & Oliveira, L. X. (2016). Gender performativity in media culture. *Interin Journal*, 21(2), 82–99.

D'Andrea, T. (2018). Contexto histórico e artístico de produção do fenômeno Racionais MC's. *Música Popular em Revista*, 5(1), 95–112.

Dapieve, A. (1995). *Brock*, São Paulo: 34.

De Marchi, L. (2006a). Indústria Fonográfica e a Nova Produção Independente. *Comunicação, Mídia e Consumo*, 3, 167–182.

De Marchi, L. (2006b). Do marginal ao empreendedor. *ECO-Pós*, 9(1), 121–140.

De Marchi, L. (2016). *A destruição criadora da indústria fonográfica brasileira 1999–2009*, Rio de Janeiro: Folio Digital.

De Marchi, L. (2023). *A indústria fonográfica digital*, Rio de Janeiro: Mauad X.

Dias, O. E. (1990). *Mathieu André Reichert*, Brasília: Universidade de Brasília.

Dias, M. T. (2000). *Os donos da voz*, São Paulo: Boitempo.

Dias, C. E. (2017). "Villa-Lobos, Antônio Carlos Jobim e Edu Lobo," PhD Dissertation, Universidade Federal de Minas Gerais, Belo Horizonte.

Diniz, A. (2007). *O Rio Musical de Anacleto de Medeiros*, Rio de Janeiro: Zahar.

Dreifuss, R. A. (1981). *1964: a conquista do Estado, ação política, poder e golpe de classe*, Petrópolis: Vozes.

Dunn, C. (2001). *Brutality Garden*, Chapel Hill: University of North Carolina.

Elias, P. H. D. M. R. (2015). "A canção tropicalista," Master Thesis, Universidade Federal de Minas Gerais, Belo Horizonte.

Fernandes, F. (1975). *A revolução burguesa no Brasil*, Rio de Janeiro, Zahar.

Fernandes, D. C. (2011). A nova ortodoxia do samba paulista. *Desigualdade & Diversidade – Revista de Ciências Sociais da PUC-Rio*, 8, 225–252.

Fernandes, D. C. & Pulici, C. M. (2016). Gosto musical e pertencimento social. *Tempo Social*, 28(2), 131–160.

Ferreira, J. & Castro Gomes, A. (2016). *1964*, Rio de Janeiro: Civilização Brasileira.

Franceschi, H. M. (2002). *A Casa Edison e seu tempo*, Rio de Janeiro: Sarapuí.

Freire, V. L. B. & Augusto, E. S. (2014). Sobre flores e canhões. *Per Musi*, 29, 220–230.

Freyre, G. (2003). *Casa-grande & senzala*, 48 ªed., São Paulo: Global.

Furtado, C. (2007). *Formação econômica do Brasil*, 34 ªed., São Paulo: Cia das Letras.

Garcia, W. (1999). *Bim Bom*, São Paulo: Paz e Terra.

Garson, M. (2015). *Jovem Guarda*, PhD Dissertation, Universidade de São Paulo, USP.

Gava, J. E. (2002). *A linguagem harmônica da Bossa Nova*, São Paulo: UNESP.

Giron, A. (2001). *Mário Reis*, São Paulo: Editora, p. 34.

Gomes, M. S. (2010). "Samba-Jazz aquém e além da Bossa Nova," PhD dissertation, Universidade de Campinas, Campinas.

Gomes, L. F. S. (2017). "Stan Getz e a Bossa Nova (1962–1964)," Master Thesis, Universidade do Estado de Santa Catarina, Florianópolis.

Gonçalves, C. K. (2013). *Música em 78 rotações*, São Paulo: Alameda.

Guerreiro, G. (2000). *A trama dos tambores*, São Paulo: Editora, p. 34.

Guerreiro do Amaral, P. M. (2014). Cosmopolitanism and the stigma of tecno-brega music. In Ulhôa, M. T., Azevedo, C. and Trotta, F., eds., *Made in Brazil*. New York: Routledge, pp. 110–120.

Guimarães, V. (2014). A passeata contra a guitarra e a "autêntica" música brasileira. In C. Rodrigues, T. Luca and V. Guimarães., orgs., *Identidades brasileiras*. São Paulo: Editora UNESP, pp. 145–173.

Gumes, N. V., Garson, M. & Argôlo, M. (2023). "Por acaso eu não sou uma mulher?" *Pagu*, 67, 1–19.

Herschmann, M. (2000). *O Funk e o Hip-Hop Invadem a Cena*, Rio de Janeiro: UFRJ.

Herschmann, M. (2010). *Indústria da música em transição*, São Paulo: Estação das Letras e Cores.

Homem de Mello, Z. (2003). *A Era dos Festivais*, São Paulo: Editora, p. 34.

Honneth, A. (1996). *The Struggle for Recognition*, Cambridge, MA: MIT Press.

Jango. (1984). Directed by Sílvio Tendler. Brazil: Caliban.

Janotti Jr., J. & Sá, S. P. (2019). Revisitando a noção de gênero musical em tempos de cultura musical digital. *Galáxia*, 41(1), 128–139.

Kühl, P. M. (2014). A música e suas histórias na obra de Araújo Porto-Alegre. In Kovensky, J. and Squeff, L., eds., *Araújo Porto-Alegre*. São Paulo: IMS, pp. 163–178.

Laus, E. (1998). A capa de disco no Brasil. *Arcos Design*, 1, 102–126.

Leme, M. N. (2003). *Que Tchan é Esse?* São Paulo: Annablume.

Leme, M. N. (2004). "Mercado editorial e música impressa no Rio de Janeiro (século XIX)" I Seminário Brasileiro sobre Livro e História Editorial. Casa de Rui Barbosa, Rio de Janeiro, November 8–11. Niterói: UFF, pp. 1–16.

Leme, M. N. (2006). "E 'saíram à luz' as novas coleções de polcas, modinhas, lundus etc.," PhD dissertation, Universidade Federal Fluminense, Niterói.

Lemos, R. & Castro, O. (2008). *Tecnobrega*, Rio de Janeiro: Aeroplano.

Lima, J. G. de. (2013). "Configurações e reconfigurações da canção brasileira (do final do século XVIII à década de 1930)", PhD Dissertation, Universidade Federal do Paraná, Curitiba.

Magaldi, C. (2004). *Music in Imperial Rio de Janeiro: European Culture in a Tropical Milieu*. Lanham, Md.: The Scarecrow Press.

Marcondes, M. A. (ed.). (1998). *Enciclopédia da Música Brasileira, Popular, Erudita e Folclórica*, São Paulo: Publifolha.

Mário, F. (1986). *Como fazer um disco independente*, Petrópolis: Editora Vozes.

Martins, F. (2022). *Quem foi que inventou o Brasil? v. 0*, Curitiba: Kotter Editorial.

Martius, C. F. P. von. (1844). Como se escreve a história do Brasil. *Revista do Instituto Histórico e Geográfico Brasileiro*, 6(24), 381–403.

Matos, C. (1999). Poesia popular e literatura nacional. *Revista do Patrimônio Histórico e Artístico Nacional*, 28, 14–39.

McCann, B. (2004). *Hello, Hello Brazil! Popular Music in the Making of Modern Brazil*. Durham: Duke University Press.

McGowan, C. & Pessanha, R. (1991). *The Brazilian Sound*, New York: Billboard Books.

Medeiros, J. (2021). *Roberto Carlos: Por isso essa voz tamanha*, São Paulo: Todavia.

Mello e Souza, G. (2003). *O Tupi e o Alaúde*, São Paulo: Duas Cidades; 34.

Mendonça, L. F. M. (2019). Legados do mangue. *Música Popular em Revista*, 6(2), p. 72–94.

Midani, A. (2008). *Música, ídolos e poder*, Rio de Janeiro: Nova Fronteira.

Middleton, R. (1990). *Studying Popular Music*, Buckingham: Open University Press.

Miranda, M. R. O. de. (2019). "Viaduto de Madureira", Master Thesis, Universidade Federal Fluminense, Rio de Janeiro.

Miranda, D. (2022). *Tempo de festa X tempo do trabalho: carnavalização na belle époque tropical*, 2nd ed. São Paulo: Editora Dialética.

Monteiro. M. (2006). Música na Corte do Brasil. In Ministério das Relações Exteriores, *Textos do Brasil*, Ministério, Brasília, 12, 33–39.

Monteiro. M. (2008). *A construção do gosto*, Rio de Janeiro: Ateliê Editorial.

Moraes, André. (2020). Viola brasileira, qual delas? *Revista da Tulha*, 6(1), 9–35.

Morelli, Rita C. L. (2008). O campo da MPB e o mercado moderno de música no Brasil. *ArtCultura*, 10(16), 87–101.

Morelli, R. C. L. (2009). *Indústria fonográfica*, Campinas: Unicamp.

Napolitano, M. (2001). *Seguindo a canção*, São Paulo: Annablume.

Napolitano, M. (2002). *História e música*, Belo Horizonte: Autêntica.

Napolitano, M. (2010). A MPB na era do rádio. In A. P. G. Ribeiro, I. Sacramento and M. Roxo, orgs., *História da televisão no Brasil*. Rio de Janeiro: Contexto, pp. 85–106.

Napolitano, M. (2022). O longo modernismo. *Revista Vórtex*, 10(3), 1–23.

Needell, J. D. (1987). *A tropical Belle Époque*, Cambridge: Cambridge University Press.

Nestrovski, L. (2013). "Sambop." Master Thesis, Universidade Federal do Estado do Rio de Janeiro, Rio de Janeiro.

Neves, J. M. (2008). *Música Brasileira Contemporânea*. 2ª ed., rev. by Gandelman, S., Rio de Janeiro: Contra Capa.

Nicolau Netto, M. (2009). *Música brasileira e identidade nacional na mundialização*, São Paulo: Anna Blume.

Nieborg, D. B. & Poell, T. (2018). The platformization of cultural production. *New Media & Society*, 20(11), 4275–4292.

Nunes, M. F. (1997). "O Turbante do faraó", Master Thesis, Universidade Federal de Santa Catarina, Florianópolis.

Olsen, D. & Sheehy, D. (eds.). (1998). *The Garland Encyclopedia of World Music*, Vol. 2: South America, Mexico, Central America, and the Caribbean. New York: Garland.

Ortiz, R. (1988). *A moderna tradição brasileira*, São Paulo: Brasiliense.

Paes, A. (2012). "Almirante e O pessoal da velha guarda," Master thesis, Universidade Federal do Estado do Rio de Janeiro, Rio de Janeiro.

Palombini, C. (2009). Soul brasileiro e funk carioca. *OPUS*, 15(1), 37–61.

Paranhos, A. (2014). "Entre a luta armada e as liberdades democráticas." VIII Congresso Português de Sociologia/40 anos de democracia(s). Évora, Portugal. Lisboa: Associação Portuguesa de Sociologia/APS, pp. 1–7.

Paranhos, A. (2021). Entre os passos do samba e o compasso da ditadura, *Música Popular em Revista*, 8, 1–23.

Peixoto, L. F. L. & Sebadelhe, J. O. (2016). *1976 Movimento Black Rio*, Rio de Janeiro: José Olympio.

Pereira, I. S. (2010). Axé-Axé. *Revista África e Africanidades*, 2(8), 1–6.

Perrone, C. A. (1985). From Noigandres to "Milagre Da Alegria." *Latin American Music Review*, 6(1), 58–79.

Perrone, C. A. & Dunn, C. (eds.). (2001). *Brazilian Popular Music and Globalization*, Gainesville: University Press of Florida.

Poell, T., Nieborg, D. B. & Duffy, B. E. (2022). *Platforms and Cultural Production*, Cambridge: Polity.

Porto-Alegre, M. de A. (1836). Ideias sobre a música. *Nitheroy*, 1, 160–183.

Prestes Filho, L. C. (coord.). (2005). *Cadeia produtiva da economia da música*, Rio de Janeiro: Instituto Gênesis/PUC-RJ.

Pro-Música Brasil. (2022). *Mercado Fonográfico Brasileiro 2021*, Rio de Janeiro: Pro-Música Brasil.

Reis, D. A. (2014). *Ditadura e democracia no Brasil*, Rio de Janeiro: Zahar.

Ribeiro, A. P. G., Sacramento, I. & Roxo, M. (Orgs.). (2010). *História da televisão no Brasil*, Rio de Janeiro: Contexto.

Ridenti, M. (2000). *Em busca do povo brasileiro*, Rio de Janeiro: Record.

Romero, S. (1902). *História da literatura brasileira*, Rio de Janeiro: H. Garnier.

Root, D. (2023). *Grove Music Online*, Oxford: Oxford Music Online.

Sá, S. P. (2021). *Música pop-periférica brasileira: videoclipes, performances e tretas na cultura digital*, Curitiba: Appris.

Sá, S. P. de. (2007). Funk carioca. *E-Compós*, 10, 1–18.

Sandroni, C. (2004). Adeus à MPB. In B. Cavalcante, H. Starling and J. Eisenberg, orgs., *Decantando a República*. Rio de Janeiro: Nova Fronteira, v. 1, pp. 25–35.

Sandroni, C. (2012). *Feitiço decente: transformações do samba no Rio de Janeiro (1917–1933)*. 2 ªed., Rio de Janeiro: Zahar.

Santos, A., Barbalho, G., Severiano, J. & Azevedo, M. A. de. (1982). *Discografia brasileira em 78 rpm*, 5 vols. Rio de Janeiro: Funarte.

Santos, C. de O. (2014). "Forró desordeiro," PhD Dissertation, Universidade Federal do Estado do Rio de Janeiro, Rio de Janeiro.

Santos, A. D. dos. (2019). Revolução à meia-luz: trocas políticas e estéticas na parceria entre Vinicius de Moraes e Antônio Carlos "Tom" Jobim. *OPUS*, 25(3), 94–109.

Saraiva, J. M. (2007). "A invenção do sambajazz," Master Thesis, PUC-Rio, Rio de Janeiro.

Saraiva, J. M. (2020). "Diálogos transatlânticos," PhD Dissertation, Universidade Federal do Estado do Rio de Janeiro, Rio de Janeiro.

Saroldi, L. C. & Moreira, S. V. (1988). *Rádio Nacional: o Brasil em Sintonia*, São Paulo: Martins Fontes.

Scott, D. (2008). *Sounds of the Metropolis*, New York: Oxford University Press.

Sevcenko, N. (2010). *A revolta da vacina*, São Paulo: Cosac Naify.

Severiano, J. (2013). *Uma história da música popular brasileira*, São Paulo: Editora, p. 34.

Sheperd, J., Horn, D. & Laing, D., eds. (2003). *Continuum Encyclopedia of Popular Music of the World*, London: Bloomsbury.

Soares, T. (2014). Building sound & fury pictures. *Contemporânea*, 12(2), 323–339.

Sodré, M. (1998). *Samba, o dono do corpo*, Rio de Janeiro: Mauad X.

Spix, J. B. von & Martius, K. F. P. von. (2017). *Viagem pelo Brasil: 1817–1820*, Brasília: Senado Federal.

Tatit, L. (1996). *O Cancionista*, São Paulo: Edusp.

Tinhorão, J. R. (1981). *Música popular*, São Paulo: Ática.

Tinhorão, J. R. (2012). *História social da música popular brasileira*, São Paulo: Editora, p. 34.

Tinhorão, J. R. (2013). *Pequena história da música popular segundo seus gêneros*, São Paulo: Editora, p. 34.

Torres, F. H. A. (2015). "Bossa Nova fora do eixo," Master Thesis, Universidade do Estado de Santa Catarina.

Trotta, F. (2011). *O samba e suas fronteiras*, Rio de Janeiro: UFRJ.

Trotta, F. da C. (2014). *No Ceará não tem disso não*, Rio de Janeiro: Folio Digital.

Tupinambá de Ulhôa, M. (2020). "Triple-time Modinha." In K. Holtsträter & T. Widmaier, eds., *Lied und populäre Kultur / Song and Popular Culture*. Münster: Waxmann Verlag, pp. 151–172.

Ulhôa, M. T. (1999). Música Sertaneja e Globalização. In Torres, R., ed., *Música Popular en América Latina*. Santiago: Fondart, pp. 47–60.

Ulhôa, M. T. (2000). Música romântica in Montes Claros. *British Journal for Ethnomusicology*, 9(1), 11–40.

Ulhôa, M. T. (2004). Let me sing my BRock. In D. P. Hernandez, H. F. L'Hoeste and E. Zolov, eds., *Rockin' las Américas*. Pittsburgh: University of Pittsburgh Press, pp. 200–219.

Ulhôa, M. T. (2010). "Bolero, Bossa Nova y Filin." III Congreso Internacional Música, Identidad y Cultura en el Caribe. Santiago de los Caballeros: Instituto de Estudios Caribeños, pp. 515–522.

Ulhôa, M. (2011). Lundu e prosódia musical. In Herculano, A., Abreu, M., Ulhôa, M. & Velloso, M., eds., *Música e história no longo século XIX*, Rio de Janeiro: Fundação Casa de Rui Barbosa, pp. 69–95.

Ulhôa, M. T. (2021). Música mecânica nos oitocentos no Brasil. *MusiMid*, 2(1), 11–29.

Ulhôa, M. (2022). "Repensando a música popular no Brasil: a noção de popular no século XIX." XXXII Congresso da ANPPOM. Natal, October 17–21. Brasília: ANPPOM, pp. 1–10.

Ulhôa, M. T. & Costa-Lima Neto, L. (2015). Cosmoramas, lundus e caxuxas no Rio de Janeiro (1821–1850). *Revista Brasileira de Música*, 28, 33–61.

Ulhôa, M. & Pereira, S. L. (2016). *Canção romântica*, Rio de Janeiro: Folio Digital.

Underwood, D. (2002). *Oscar Niemeyer e o modernismo de formas livres no Brasil*, São Paulo: Cosac Naify.

Vargas, H. & Carvalho, N. (2021). A noção de pós-gênero. *Comunicação & Informação*, 24(1), 1–20.

Vaz, G. N. (1988). *História da música independente*, São Paulo: Brasiliense.

Vedana, H. (2006). *A Elétrica e os discos Gaúchos*, Porto Alegre: SCP.

Veloso, M. & Madeira, A. (1999). *Leituras Brasileiras*. São Paulo: Paz e Terra.

Vianna, H. (1988). *O Mundo Funk Carioca*. Rio de Janeiro: Jorge Zahar Editor.

Vianna, H. (2004). *O Mistério do Samba*, Rio de Janeiro: Jorge Zahar/UFRJ.

Vicente, E. (2014). *Da vitrola ao iPod*, São Paulo: Alameda.

Vilarino, R. C. (2006). *A MPB em movimento*, São Paulo: Olho d'Água.

Volpe, M. A. (2022). A música na imprensa periódica. In F. M. de Barros Júnior & R. F. dos S. Ferreira, orgs., *Periódicos & Literatura: aproximações*, Rio de Janeiro: Fundação Biblioteca Nacional, pp. 121–180.

Wisnik, J. M. (2022). A República Musical Modernista. In Gênese Andrade, org., *Modernismos 1922-2022*, 1st ed. São Paulo: Companhia das Letras, pp. 171–195.

Zan, J. R. (2001). Música popular brasileira, indústria cultural e identidade. *EccoS Rev. Cient.*, UNINOVE, 1(3), 105–122.

Cambridge Elements ☰

Popular Music

Rupert Till
University of Huddersfield

Rupert Till is Professor of Music at the University of Huddersfield, UK, Associate Dean International in his faculty and Director of the Confucius Institute at the University. He has research interests in popular music and sound archaeology. He is Chair of the International Association for the Study of Popular Music IASPM, and a committee member of the UK and Ireland Branch. He directed Huddersfield activities within the EU funded European Music Archaeology Project, (2013-18), and has been Principal Investigator for two AHRC/EPSRC grants. He studied composition with Gavin Bryars, Christopher Hobbs, Katharine Norman, and George Nicholson. He continues to write electronica and perform under the name "Professor Chill".

About the Series

Elements in Popular Music showcases exciting original work from across this lively, diverse and expanding field. It embraces all aspects of popular music studies, from music history and ethnomusicology to composition, songwriting and performance, and the music industries, recording and production. Its content will also appeal to scholars and students of media studies and cultural studies exploring topics such as fandom, celebrity, screen studies and music journalism. The study of popular music often involves crossing disciplinary boundaries and drawing on a variety of empirical and creative methodologies to illuminate topics such as identity and embodiment, power and resistance. Each Element in the series is illustrated by engaging case studies that will attract a broad range of readers from the academy and beyond.

Popular Music